ESSENTIAL ASSESSMENT CONCEPTS FOR TEACHERS AND ADMINISTRATORS

JAMES H. MCMILLAN

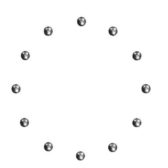

EXPERTS IN ASSESSMENT

SERIES EDITORS
THOMAS R. GUSKEY AND ROBERT J. MARZANO

CORWIN PRESS, INC.
A Sage Publications Company
Thousand Oaks, California

For information:

 Corwin Press, Inc.
A Sage Publications Company
2455 Teller Road
Thousand Oaks, California 91320
E-mail: order@corwinpress.com

Sage Publications Ltd.
6 Bonhill Street
London EC2A 4PU
United Kingdom

Sage Publications India Pvt. Ltd.
M-32 Market
Greater Kailash I
New Delhi 110 048 India

Printed in the United States of America

Library of Congress Cataloging-in-Publication Data

McMillan, James H.
    Essential assessment concepts for teachers and administrators / by James H. McMillan
        p. cm. — (Experts in assessment kit; v. 1)
    Includes bibliographical references and index.
        ISBN 0-8039-6839-6 (cloth: alk. paper) — ISBN 0-8039-6840-X (pbk.: alk. paper)
        1. Educational tests and measurements. 2. Grading and marking (students)   I. Title.   II. Series
        LB3051 .M4624992 2000
        371.26—dc21   99. 050874

This book is printed on acid-free paper.

01 02 03 04 05 06 10 9 8 7 6 5 4 3 2 1

Production Editor: Astrid Virding
Editorial Assistant: Catherine Kantor
Typesetter: Rebecca Evans
Cover Designer: Tracy E. Miller

ESSENTIAL ASSESSMENT CONCEPTS FOR TEACHERS AND ADMINISTRATORS

EXPERTS IN ASSESSMENT

SERIES EDITORS
THOMAS R. GUSKEY AND ROBERT J. MARZANO

JUDITH ARTER, JAY MCTIGHE
SCORING RUBRICS IN THE CLASSROOM: USING PERFORMANCE CRITERIA FOR ASSESSING AND IMPROVING STUDENT PERFORMANCE

JANE M. BAILEY, THOMAS R. GUSKEY
IMPLEMENTING STUDENT-LED CONFERENCES

THOMAS R. GUSKEY, JANE M. BAILEY
DEVELOPING GRADING AND REPORTING SYSTEMS FOR STUDENT LEARNING

EDWARD KIFER
LARGE-SCALE ASSESSMENT: DIMENSIONS, DILEMMAS, AND POLICY

ROBERT J. MARZANO
DESIGNING A NEW TAXONOMY OF EDUCATIONAL OBJECTIVES

JAMES H. MCMILLAN
ESSENTIAL ASSESSMENT CONCEPTS FOR TEACHERS AND ADMINISTRATORS

JEFFREY K. SMITH, LISA F. SMITH, RICHARD DE LISI
NATURAL CLASSROOM ASSESSMENT: DESIGNING SEAMLESS INSTRUCTION AND ASSESSMENT

ISBN 0-7619-7756-2 (7-BOOK PAPER EDITION)
ISBN 0-7619-7757-0 (7-BOOK LIBRARY EDITION)

Contents

Series Editors' Introduction

Standards, assessment, accountability, and grading—these are the issues that dominated discussions of education in the 1990s. Today, they are at the center of every modern education reform effort. As educators turn to the task of implementing these reforms, they face a complex array of questions and concerns that little in their background or previous experience has prepared them to address. This series is designed to help in that challenging task.

In selecting the authors, we went to individuals recognized as true experts in the field. The ideas of these scholar-practitioners have already helped shape current discussions of standards, assessment, accountability, and grading. But equally important, their work reflects a deep understanding of the complexities involved in implementation. As they developed their books for this series, we asked them to extend their thinking, to push the edge, and to present new perspectives on what should be done and how to do it. That is precisely what they did. The books they crafted provide not only cutting-edge perspectives but also practical guidelines for successful implementation.

We have several goals for this series. First, that it be used by teachers, school leaders, policy makers, government officials, and all those concerned with these crucial aspects of education reform. Second, that it helps broaden understanding of the complex issues involved in standards, assessment, accountability, and grading. Third, that it leads to more thoughtful policies and programs. Fourth, and most important, that it helps accomplish the basic goal for which all reform initiatives are intended—namely, to enable all students to learn excellently and to gain the many positive benefits of that success.

— *Thomas R. Guskey*
Robert J. Marzano
Series Editors

Preface

This is a book that I have wanted to write for a long time. After more than 25 years in the education profession, I am convinced that a solid foundation in assessment concepts and principles is essential to effective teaching. I've seen how sound assessment can motivate students and enhance learning, and, especially recently, I have seen how assessment can be misused and harmful. Clearly, assessment is at the forefront of reform in education. Now, more than ever, those conducting assessments and using results need to be well-informed about what we have learned through many decades and about what standards guide our profession.

My intent in this first volume in The Experts on Assessment Kit is to present essential assessment concepts in a concise manner that can be understood and applied by teachers, administrators, and other school personnel. Policymakers, as well, will find the content helpful in making assessment-related decisions. To accomplish this, I have organized the chapters around major assessment topics. The first chapter provides an introduction to assessment terminology and the connection between assessment and instruction. The next three chapters introduce validity, reliability, and fairness, topics that are integral to developing high-quality assessments and using them appropriately. Chapter 5 reviews essential numerical concepts, and Chapter 6 discusses important principles of standardized testing, including standards-based standardized testing.

I want to thank the series coeditors, Tom Guskey and Bob Marzano, for their support and helpful feedback in the preparation of the manuscript, as well as Corwin acquisitions editor Alice Foster. I am especially grateful to Judy Singh for her careful editing.

About the Author

James H. McMillan is Professor of Educational Studies at Virginia Commonwealth University in Richmond, Virginia, where he teaches educational research and assessment courses and directs the Research and Evaluation Track of the Ph.D. in Education program. He is also Director of the Metropolitan Educational Research Consortium, a partnership of Virginia Commonwealth University and seven Richmond-area school divisions that conducts and disseminates action research. His current research interests include classroom and large-scale assessment. He has recently published *Classroom Assessment: Principles and Practice for Effective Instruction* and has authored three educational research methods textbooks. He has published numerous articles in journals, including the *American Educational Research Journal,* the *Journal of Educational Psychology, Contemporary Educational Psychology,* and *Educational Measurement: Issues and Practice.* He is currently serving as President of the American Educational Research Association Classroom Assessment Special Interest Group.

CHAPTER 1

Integrating Assessment With Teaching and Learning

I t wasn't too long ago that I was a student taking a "tests and measurement" course. We spent most of our time learning how to construct objective classroom tests (multiple-choice, matching, and true-false) and how to interpret standardized test scores. But I really didn't see much relevance to teaching or to student learning. The emphasis was on testing after instruction to determine grades and on using standardized test scores to see how students compared with other students in the nation. I learned that measurement was separate from instruction, something that was done to document or audit student achievement. Today, however, new theories of learning, motivation, and instruction have led to a reconceptualization of measurement concepts, ideas, and principles. There is now realization that assessment, more broadly conceived, is an essential part of instruction and should be viewed as a tool not only to document learning but also to enhance learning. Whether the assessment is focused on what occurs in the classroom or on externally mandated standardized tests, teachers now know how to effectively integrate assessment with teaching and learning so that it enhances learning and the attainment of overall educational goals.

Recently, I had an opportunity to interview some teachers about their classroom assessments and grading. Here is what a few of them said:

- To me, grades are extremely secondary to the whole process of what we do. I have goals to what I want to teach, and I use assessment so that I know what I need to work on, what people have mastered, and what they haven't.

- I've changed to using more group assessments. If you really want a student to learn, the student has to be actively engaged, and doing group work. I find that works best. You can just see the lights go on with the kids.

1

- When they come in, you give them a pop quiz. It reinforces what they learned the day before.

- It'll go back to the goal I have: Try to meet the needs, interests, and ca-pabilities of the children. If you don't have a variety of assessments, you're not really focusing on what the students' abilities are.

- I always assess early on to see what people know so that I could split groups as needed. I am a real stickler for assessing only to find out what people know and what they've learned.

- Assessments where they actually have to show me some work or write about them are most valuable for informing me about what students know. Because it's then that you know that they understood every pro-cess. That tells you a lot more about a student than just grading a sheet of answers.

As you can see, these teachers, who represent a range of experience and subject matter, think about classroom assessments and grading as components of instruction. They don't separate "testing" and grading from instruction. Rather, they see instruction and assessment as integrated aspects of teaching, each depending on the other. This is an important departure point for decid-ing what constitutes "essential measurement concepts." My view is that what is most basic to assessment is what is fundamental to understanding and en-hancing student learning. After all, isn't this what education is all about?

Although classroom assessment focuses on what teachers do daily to in-fluence student learning, standardized testing can also be used to enhance student performance. Ironically, at the same time that increased emphasis has been placed on classroom assessments, standardized tests are being used with greater frequency to verify student performance and accredit schools. Consequently, teachers and administrators need a thorough understanding of fundamental concepts and principles of both classroom assessment and standardized testing to effectively apply these tools to improve student achievement.

In this chapter, I will take you through what I consider essential concepts that link assessment, instruction, and learning. I'll need to define some terms to lay the groundwork for later applications but will spend most of the chapter showing how assessment, in its many forms, and instruction and learning are inexorably intertwined.

The Role of Assessment in Teaching

With some reflection, it isn't hard to see how assessment is essential to teach-ing. Teaching is conceptualized today as a process of effective decision mak-

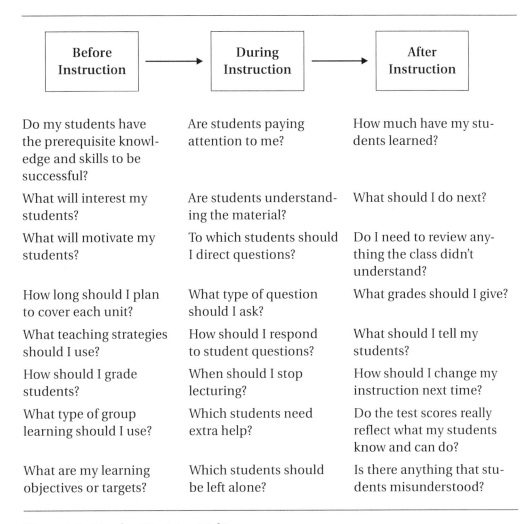

Figure 1.1. Teacher Decision Making

ing. This includes deciding what to teach, how to teach it, how long to teach, whether to group students, what questions to ask, what follow-up questions to ask, what to review, when to review, and so forth. Figure 1.1 illustrates the nature of decisions according to when the decisions are made—before, during, or after instruction. This is a useful way to think about teacher decision making because it organizes the decisions by the sequence teachers use.

Each decision that is made needs to be based on something. Typically, teachers use their experience, logical reasoning, and tradition, among other sources of knowledge, to make their decisions. Assessment of students is critical because effective decision making is based to some extent on the ability of teachers to understand their students and to match actions with accurate assessments. Can you imagine a doctor deciding on a prescription without a complete understanding of the patient? Likewise, teachers need to understand students before they can choose instructional methods and give students grades. In other words, effective teachers include assessment as a source of information for decision making.

What Is Assessment?

Although there are different definitions of assessment in the literature, the one by Peter Airasian (1997) is especially good: "Assessment is the process of collecting, synthesizing, and interpreting information to aid in decision making" (p. 3). I like this definition because it conveys clearly and succinctly different aspects that make up the complete process of "assessment." This is a contemporary view. In the past, assessment tended to be equated more or less with testing and the simple gathering of information. The broader, more inclusive, definition is better because it places such tasks as making up a test, administering it, and scoring the results in a larger context that includes interpretation and use of the results.

I find it helpful to think about assessment as having four major, sequential components: purpose, method of measurement or description, evaluation, and use (see Figure 1.2). The next sections consider each one.

Purpose

There are many reasons to assess students. Teachers want to know how much students understand before they begin a unit of instruction, how much students are progressing in their understanding during instruction, and how much students have learned at the end of a unit. Special education teachers need assessments to prescribe specific instructional strategies. Principals want to know how students in their school score on standardized tests. Parents want assessment information to see how well their children are doing in school. Policymakers need assessment data to make judgments about the quality of education that students receive. Colleges need student scores on admissions tests to make admissions decisions.

Assessment begins, then, with identification of the specific purpose for collecting and interpreting the information. Once the purpose has been identified, appropriate methods for gathering and synthesizing the information can be identified. What works well for one purpose may not work well for another. This is an important lesson about assessment: *The nature of the assessment method should follow from the intended purpose.*

In thinking about purpose, it is helpful to differentiate classroom assessment from large-scale standardized assessment (school district, state, and na-

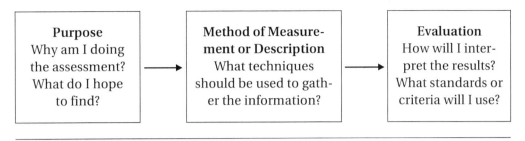

Figure 1.2. Major Components of Classroom Assessment

SOURCE: Adapted from *Classroom Assessment: Principles and Practice for Effective Instruction* (2nd ed.), by J. H. McMillan, in press, Boston: Allyn & Bacon. Copyright © by Allyn & Bacon, Incorporated. Adapted with permission.

tional assessments). Both may have the same ultimate goal, to improve student learning, but the more immediate purposes, methods, and use of results differ in significant ways. The purposes of classroom assessment are focused on teacher decision making and include the following (not a complete list):

- To identify if students have mastered a concept or skill
- To motivate students to be more engaged in learning
- To get students to learn the content in a way that stresses application and other reasoning skills
- To help develop a positive attitude about a subject
- To communicate to parents what students know and can do
- To communicate expectations to students
- To give students feedback about what they know and can do
- To show students what they need to focus on to improve their understanding
- To encourage student self-evaluation
- To determine report card grades
- To evaluate the effectiveness of instructional approaches

Standardized, large-scale assessments have different immediate purposes (not all of which are desirable):

- To evaluate the effectiveness of a new curriculum
- To identify student strengths and weaknesses
- To compare different schools or school divisions
- To evaluate teachers

From:	To:
Sole emphasis on outcomes after learning	Assessing process during learning
Isolated, disconnected facts and skills	Integrated skills
Assessing with decontextualized tasks	Assessing with contextualized tasks
Single correct answers	Many correct answers
Providing little feedback to students	Providing considerable feedback to students
Sporadic assessment	Continual assessment
Controlling and documenting	Motivating
Demonstrating knowledge with unauthentic tasks	Demonstrating knowledge with authentic tasks
Knowing and simple understanding	Deep understanding and application
Memorization	Thinking

Figure 1.3. Recent Trends in the Purpose of Classroom Assessments

- To provide information for school accreditation
- To see how students as a group do in comparison with a national sample of students
- To evaluate principals
- To determine if students are meeting state or national "standards"
- To determine how to group students
- To allocate resources
- To identify students with special needs

Once the purpose is identified, a critical question needs to be asked, namely, *What evidence is needed to provide the best information to meet the stated purpose?* This seemingly simple question lies at the heart of high-quality decision making. There are many choices in the nature of the evidence. Let's look at an example with classroom assessment. Suppose you are a teacher and have identified the following purpose: "to give students feedback to enable them to improve their skill in multiplying fractions." Now, what type of assessment will best meet this purpose? Should the assessment be done in class or at home? Should a quiz use multiple-choice questions or constructed-response questions (for which students show their work)? Should students get credit for knowing the process but not getting the correct answer because of faulty

Table 1.1 Differences Between Classroom and Standardized, Large-Scale Assessment

Classroom Assessment	Standardized, Large-Scale Assessment
Focused on individual students	Focused on groups of students
Conducted before, during, and after instruction	Conducted before and after instruction
Teacher-made	Made by outside "experts"
Tailored to individual classes	Same items for all students
Immediate individualized feedback to students	Delayed general feedback to students
May be timed or untimed	Usually timed
Given continuously	Given sporadically
Tends to cover short units	Tends to cover a large domain of content
Compares scores with levels of performance	Tends to report scores compared with other students
Weak technically	Strong technically
Used for grading students and improvement	Used for teacher and school accountability

arithmetic? I think that assessments done in class (where parents can't help) that require students to show their work would provide stronger evidence of what students can do than would homework or multiple-choice tests. The former would give the teacher an opportunity to diagnose misunderstandings to pinpoint immediate feedback that is individualized and specific to the task. Thus, the constructed-response items meet the stated purpose much better than would homework or a multiple-choice test. This example illustrates an important trend in classroom assessment: *There is as much emphasis on how the assessment can improve student learning as there is on using the assessment to document student learning.* This trend and others are summarized in Figure 1.3.

An important distinction to keep in mind between the purposes of classroom assessment and standardized, large-scale assessment is that classroom assessment is focused on the individual student and how to provide the best information to maximize student learning in a particular classroom. Large-scale assessment, on the other hand, emphasizes group data, typically at the school, district, or state level. Other differences are summarized in Table 1.1.

Method of Measurement or Description

After the purpose of assessment has been identified, a method of measuring the trait or skill of interest needs to be selected. Assessment methods can be divided into two major categories: those that use measurement and those that use nonnumerical description. The term *measurement* is used to describe the process by which traits, attributes, performance, behavior, and characteristics (I'll use the single term *trait* to refer to all of these) are *differentiated* by assigning different numbers to represent the degree to which the trait is possessed by or demonstrated by an individual. This is essentially asking *how much* of something is observed and using some scale to quantify the extent of it. Thus, teachers administer tests and score them to record the measurement of the trait, for example, a "70" or "94." Similarly, on a standardized test, a score may be reported as a raw score of the number of items answered correctly, the percentage of items answered correctly, a "standard" score, or a percentile rank. In each case, numbers are generated from some type of test or performance to represent the degree to which the trait is present. This is called *quantitative* assessment.

Traits are also differentiated through the use of verbal descriptions, rather than numbers. This is termed *qualitative* assessment. Words, rather than numbers, are used to differentiate the traits. For example, teachers may describe performance by pointing out what was included, appropriately, and what was missing. Here are two illustrations of this type of description:

> "John, you have used the correct formula to solve the problem but did not subtract accurately."

> "Kim, the project you submitted demonstrated a complete understanding of different types of trees. Your conclusions would be better if you mentioned all types of trees."

Many newer types of assessments describe different levels or degrees of performance verbally and then assign numbers to each level, for example:

1	2	3	4
Has a severely limited range of complex thinking skills for managing complex tasks	Demonstrates ability in a number of complex thinking processes but does not have a full complement of skills for managing complex issues	Demonstrates competency in a number of complex thinking processes and usually applies the processes effectively	Demonstrates mastery of a variety of complex thinking processes and consistently applies the processes effectively

Table 1.2 Classifying Methods of Assessment

	Traditional	*Alternative*
Selected-response	Multiple-choice	Student self-assessment
	True-false	
	Matching	
	Binary-choice	
	Structured observation	
	Structured interview	
	Surveys	
Constructed-response	Sentence completion	Performance assessment
	Short answer	Authentic assessment
	Essay	Portfolio assessment
	Anecdotal observation	Exhibitions
	Unstructured interview	Demonstrations
	Papers	Student self-assessment
	Reports	

The measurement and description process includes both the procedures for collecting information and the assigning of numbers or verbal narratives to represent different degrees of the trait.

The procedures for collecting information can vary, from something structured and formal, such as an objective test, to something unstructured and informal, such as teacher observation. Table 1.2 summarizes different types of measurement and descriptive techniques. They have been classified as *traditional* or *alternative* to highlight the changing nature of educational assessment. Traditional assessments are those that were developed to measure traits with paper-and-pencil tests, such as multiple-choice tests and essay tests. Alternative assessments refer to those that are based on a different philosophy and goal to provide a stronger link between instruction and assessment and make learning more significant. This is consistent with recent constructivist research that emphasizes the importance of constructing responses in relation to existing knowledge, as well as the recognition that effective education develops students' thinking and reasoning skills in addition to mastery of content (Cizek, 1997; Tombari & Borich, 1999). *Authentic assessments* are constructed to be consistent with what people do in situations that occur naturally outside the classroom. In *performance assessments,* students are required to demonstrate a skill or proficiency by creating, producing, or doing something. This occurs when students complete a project, give a speech, paint a picture, build a model home, or write a letter to the editor of a newspaper. Demonstrations or exhibitions are types of performance assessments. *Portfolios* are collections of student work that illustrate performance and improvement through time.

Types of measurements and descriptions can also be categorized as *selected-response* or *constructed-response* (sometimes called supply type). With selected-response items, the examinee chooses an answer from those provided, as with multiple-choice, true-false, and matching. In a constructed-response assessment, students literally construct, rather than choose, a response. Constructed-response examples include short-answer items, completing a project, and giving a speech. Sometimes, selected-response assessments are called "objective" tests, whereas constructed-response assessments may be called "subjective" tests. This difference, however, refers only to the manner in which the answers are scored. Thus, a sentence completion item is a constructed-response question, but the scoring may be primarily objective if only a single answer is correct. Other constructed-response items, such as essays, may have more than one correct response and therefore are judged subjectively.

In Table 1.2, alternative assessments are completely constructed-response, whereas traditional measurement techniques may be either selected- or constructed-response. This highlights an important trend—but not one without controversy. Some maintain that traditional assessment techniques, because they have been around a long time, are tried-and-tested methods that are both familiar and trustworthy. Others argue that these same measures cannot begin to adequately assess more important skills. The significant thing to remember is that there are advantages and disadvantages to both traditional and alternative assessments and that it is most crucial to match the type of assessment with the purpose. *Remember, begin with purpose, and, with a knowledge of assessment options, select and implement the one(s) that will provide the best evidence.* Table 1.3 summarizes some matches between type of assessment method and different purposes.

Evaluation

After the appropriate method of assessment has been administered, the numbers or descriptions that are gathered must be interpreted. The interpretation involves making a judgment about the quality of what is gathered. This is essentially an evaluation of what has been performed. By *evaluation,* I mean a judgment about the worth or value of the performance. There is an *interpretation* of what the results mean and how they can be used. Teachers typically

Table 1.3 Matching Purpose With Method of Assessment

	Method of Assessment				
Purpose	*Selected-Response*	*Essay*	*Performance Assessment*	*Oral Question*	*Observation*
Document student mastery of content	Excellent	Poor	Fair	Fair	Fair
Document student reasoning	Fair	Good	Excellent	Good	Fair
Document student skills	Fair	Fair	Excellent	Fair	Excellent
Diagnose student weaknesses	Fair	Poor	Good	Good	Good
Use for school accountability	Good	Poor	Fair	Poor	Poor
Evaluate curriculum	Good	Fair	Good	Fair	Fair
Use as a barrier test for high school graduation	Good	Poor	Fair	Fair	Poor
Motivate students	Fair	Good	Excellent	Good	Fair
Assess student perceptions and interests	Good	Poor	Fair	Good	Fair

make these evaluations on how student performance compares with the learning objective or goal. This is often referred to as a *criterion-referenced* interpretation. Performance is compared with a standard or levels of performance that have been designated.

Consider as an example the following learning objective: "Students will understand the process of photosynthesis." The teacher asks students to describe photosynthesis in two paragraphs. A criterion-referenced evaluation is made by comparing each student's response with criteria that have been identified as essential to understanding photosynthesis. If a student has clearly mastered every aspect of photosynthesis, an evaluation may be "excellent," whereas partial understanding may be termed "good." Because all students are compared with levels of understanding, the evaluation does not depend at all on how students compare with each other.

With *norm-referenced* assessments, the scores are evaluated by how students compare with each other or with some other group of students. Thus, if a student scores as well as half of the comparison group, the evaluation might be that the student has demonstrated "average" knowledge or understanding. For students who score better than most, the evaluation might be "excellent." But these interpretations do not indicate much about the actual level of knowledge or understanding. With norm-referenced assessments, evaluators need to examine the questions carefully to know the level of performance that is demonstrated, as well as the nature of the group that is used for comparison. For years, most standardized testing has reported norm-referenced scores, which are less useful for improving teaching and learning than are criterion-referenced scores.

Use

Once the information gathered has been evaluated, it is used to meet the purpose for which it was intended. That is, it is used to make decisions about students, instruction, curriculum, teachers, and schools. Classroom assessments are typically put to two uses. One is to inform the teacher about how much students know and understand so that appropriate instructional interventions can be planned and implemented to enhance learning. A second use is based on documenting what students have learned, resulting in grades and report cards to inform students, parents, and others about student progress. Standardized, large-scale assessments are put to many uses, including accrediting schools, qualifying students for graduation, and evaluating curriculum.

What is important is that the way the results are used is consistent with assessment methods and evaluations. For example, the results from constructed-response formats with criterion-referenced evaluations are best when using assessments to give informative and motivating feedback to students. Results from selected-response formats with norm-referenced evaluations are best when assessing achievement of a large body of knowledge in relation to a national sample of students.

Assessment Decision Making

As with other types of decision making, teachers are influenced by a variety of factors when they decide when and how to assess students. Recent research has found that teachers are influenced by two types of factors (McMillan, 1999b). The first is essentially internal to each teacher, consisting of teacher beliefs and values. The second is external, pressuring teachers to adopt certain assessment practices. Teacher beliefs and values that influence assessment decision making include the following:

- Philosophy of teaching (e.g., believing that all students can learn and in challenging students)

- Pulling for students (wanting students to be successful)

- Motivation and engagement (believing that motivation and engagement are essential to learning)

- Promoting student understanding (wanting students to truly understand concepts, principles, and skills, rather than merely showing rote memory or recognition)

- Accommodating individual differences among students (using different instructional strategies and assessments with students differing in aptitude, knowledge, learning style, attitudes, and other characteristics)

These teacher beliefs and values focus on what is best for student learning and provide the foundation for making assessment decisions. Thus, teachers may use constructed-response test items rather than selected-response items because the constructed-response items give a better measure of student understanding. Teachers may give extra credit to enable students to "pull up" low grades. Because of individual differences in students, teachers may use different types of assessments so that everyone has a chance of being successful. Performance assessments may be used because they motivate and engage students more effectively than multiple-choice tests.

External factors also affect how teachers assess students. These factors are not controllable. They represent reality in that they must be considered, but they may have effects that teachers may view as undesirable. External factors include the following:

- Mandated statewide or national high-stakes standardized tests (tests with consequences for students and/or teachers and schools)

- Parental pressure (e.g., demands for verification of student performance that led to a low grade)

- District grading policies (guidelines that restrict teachers to certain procedures)

- Practical constraints (e.g., number of students, time needed to grade papers, and diversity of students served)

Although teacher beliefs and values stress what is best for learning, these external pressures are usually more oriented to auditing student learning. Clearly, mandated statewide accountability testing has changed classroom assessment so that it is more aligned with the format of the statewide test. If a high-stakes test uses a multiple-choice format, then teachers are pressured to use multiple-choice classroom tests. Teachers want to be able to show parents "objective" evidence of student performance to defend grades, and district policies may restrict the nature and use of different assessments. Practical constraints limit what teachers can realistically do. Although extensive authentic performance assessments might be best, they might not be feasible in light of other instructional needs.

As you can see, teacher beliefs and values often conflict with external pressures, especially when the teacher—or administrator, for that matter—focuses on enhancing student learning, and external pressures are focused on auditing student learning. This constant tension shapes the assessment environment in a school and in classrooms and helps in understanding *why* specific assessment practices are used and the effect of those practices on student learning.

How can teachers and administrators ease the tension brought about from these two factors to result in a balanced and positive assessment environment? Here are a few suggestions.

1. Be crystal clear about *all* the educational goals of the state, district, school, and classroom teacher.

2. Gather and report evidence on all educational goals (not just the more visible state goals).

3. Consistently check the alignment between assessment purpose and method.

4. Make sure that teachers and administrators understand what it takes to generate *high-quality* assessments.

5. Avoid inappropriate uses of statewide assessments (e.g., for teacher or principal evaluations).

6. Treat teachers and administrators as professionals who need autonomy, support, and trust.

7. Don't allow statewide assessments to dominate local school practices.

Assessment Standards for Teachers and Administrators

Teachers rely on assessment to provide information that will inform and improve instruction. Because teachers play varied roles within the school, they need to be knowledgeable and competent in assessment practices that are used in these roles. In 1990, four professional organizations (the American

Association of Colleges of Teacher Education, the American Federation of Teachers, the National Council on Measurement in Education, and the National Education Association) agreed to a set of seven assessment competencies needed by teachers (*Standards*, 1990). These seven areas include the following:

1. Teachers should be skilled in choosing assessment methods that are appropriate, depending on technical adequacy, usefulness, convenience, and fairness, for instructional decisions.

2. Teachers should be skilled in developing all types of assessments.

3. Teachers should be skilled in administering, scoring, and interpreting both standardized tests and classroom assessments.

4. Teachers should be skilled in using assessment results to make decisions about individual students, instruction, curriculum, and school improvement.

5. Teachers should be skilled in developing rational, justifiable, and fair procedures for grading students.

6. Teachers should be skilled in communicating assessment results to students, parents, other lay audiences, and other educators.

7. Teachers should recognize and practice sound ethics and legal requirements.

There is also a set of guidelines for school administrators, also recently developed by four professional organizations (the National Council on Measurement in Education, the American Association of School Administrators, the National Association of Elementary School Principals, and the National Association of Secondary School Principals; Impara & Plake, 1996). Administrators should have the following 10 administrator assessment competencies:

1. Understand assessment standards for teachers.

2. Understand and apply basic precepts of assessment and measurement theory.

3. Understand different purposes of different types of assessments.

4. Understand and communicate measurement terminology.

5. Recognize appropriate and inappropriate uses of assessments and follow ethical guidelines.

6. Know how to construct appropriate and useful assessments.

7. Know how to accurately interpret and appropriately use assessment results.

8. Understand how interpretation of assessment results is moderated by student characteristics.

9. Be able to evaluate an assessment program or strategy.

10. Use computer-based assessment tools.

What is your current self-assessment of level of understanding and skill of these competencies? Together, the two lists cover a lot! Furthermore, becoming competent in these standards requires initial understanding, followed by application in which feedback can be provided to increase depth of understanding. But knowing the competencies now gives you a feel for the assessment landscape. The remaining chapters will examine more specific assessment principles that relate to most of these competencies, for both teachers and administrators. The purpose is to cover the basic, fundamental assessment concepts and principles that will equip you to be a more effective assessor and educator. This chapter has covered the overall assessment framework. The remaining chapters will fill in additional detail.

CHAPTER 2

Validity

We have seen that assessment consists of collecting, interpreting, and using information in decision making and that assessment can be used to improve instruction and enhance learning, as well as to document student performance. Thinking about assessment in this way has important implications for how a familiar concept, validity, is defined and applied. Validity is concerned with the entire process of assessment, not just the collection of scores or other information.

What Is Validity?

Validity can be defined as an overall evaluation that supports the intended interpretation, use, and consequences of the obtained scores. This evaluation is at the heart of high-quality assessment. Strong validity is demonstrated when evidence and logic suggest that the evaluation is accurate and reasonable. In other words, validity concerns the soundness, trustworthiness, or legitimacy of the inferences or claims that are made on the basis of the obtained scores. Obviously, better decisions will be made when the inferences or claims are accurate. Thus, the interpretations, uses, and consequences—not the test, instrument, or procedure used to gather the information—have some degree of validity. Often, the phrase "the validity of the test" is used, but it is more accurate to say "the validity of the inference from test scores." Clearly, validity is not a characteristic of a test or instrument that accompanies the test or instrument wherever and whenever it is administered. Tests cannot be valid; only inferences can be valid.

As shown in Figure 2.1, assessments are administered within a context or setting to obtain scores; the scores are then used to make claims, meanings, interpretations, and so forth. Thus, validity is a judgment, based on available evidence, about the accuracy and reasonableness of the claim or other use within the given context. Let's look at a couple of examples. The same steps are used for both classroom and large-scale assessments.

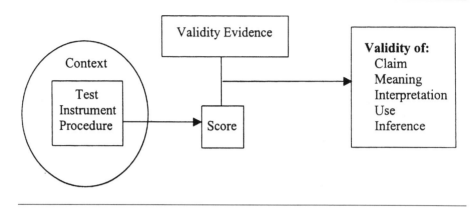

Figure 2.1. Determining Validity

Mr. Taylor decides to assign a research project to students in his math class. Students are asked to construct a model house with five rooms, with doors and windows, that will have a given inside wall space in square feet (according to scale). Each student must construct the house in class within a week. Students are graded on whether the house is complete and accurate according to scale and with respect to total square feet. Mr. Taylor believes that this is a good assessment procedure and that students with a high grade (score) have demonstrated mastery of being able to calculate square footage (evaluation). The validity questions are these: How accurate and reasonable is the conclusion that students who score high have mastered this skill? How does Mr. Taylor know?

In Greenville County, the superintendent decides to institute a new evaluation system for teachers. She decides to use student test scores from the norm-referenced, standardized test given to students each spring as an indicator of teacher effectiveness. In other words, the test *scores* are *used* to *infer* whether teachers are effective. The validity questions here are these: How reasonable is it to use standardized test scores for measuring teacher effectiveness? Is it actually true (accurate) that teachers whose students score high are more effective than teachers whose students score low?

A common misconception about validity is that it is simply "the extent to which a test measures what it is supposed, or purported, to measure." This notion suggests, erroneously, that validity is a characteristic of the test. Although the substance of the test is important for validity, substance is just one aspect that is involved in making a proper inference. Validity involves much more. For example, results from a test of student knowledge about algebra may be valid as an assessment of current competence but not valid for predicting achievement. A biology test may provide scores that could be valid for making decisions about content that needs to be retaught but invalid for inferring that students can reason or can read well. (Although this language suggests that in-

Table 2.1 Characteristics of Validity

- Validity is a matter of overall professional judgment.
- Validity refers to the accuracy of inferences, not to the test or procedure itself.
- Validity is specific to particular uses in particular contexts.
- Validity is not an "all or none" judgment but a matter of degree.
- Validity is a singular concept.
- Validity is established with different types of evidence.
- Validity is the joint responsibility of test developer and test user.

---

ferences can be valid or invalid, validity is always a matter of degree, for example, high or strong, moderate, and low or weak.)

Table 2.1 provides an overview of the nature of validity by summarizing important characteristics. In this table, one of the characteristics refers to validity as a "singular" concept. Some years ago, different types of validity were often referenced (e.g., content-related validity and criterion-related validity). Today, however, validity is considered to be a unitary idea, with different sources of validity evidence. For both large-scale and classroom assessments, test developers bear the responsibility of providing evidence that the stated uses of the test are valid. The test user, however, has ultimate responsibility for establishing validity in the particular setting in which test is used. If the use of test results differs from what has been identified by the test developer, then the local user has added responsibility for gathering appropriate evidence. For example, suppose that a state's student competency exam has been developed to ascertain student proficiency. If this test is used to evaluate teachers, this use needs to be supported by evidence gathered by the user. For most classroom tests, the teacher has the primary responsibility to gather evidence that the scores from the tests are appropriate indicators for specific uses, such as grades and instructional decisions (Whittington, 1999).

How Is Validity Determined?

Developing a strong case for validity involves a number of steps. It begins with a clear statement of the intended interpretations, claims, uses, or meanings for an assessment. (This statement typically includes a rationale for how that interpretation or meaning is related to the use of the scores.) Once the statement is complete, evidence is accumulated to support the legitimacy and accuracy of the intended use. In education, the proposed interpretation, meaning, or claim is closely tied to the content or skills being taught. Here are some examples of interpretations related to content or skills:

- The assessment will indicate whether the students have mastered multiplying fractions.
- The assessment will show how much students know about the Vietnam War.
- The assessment will show which components of experimentation students understand.
- The assessment will indicate how much students know about U.S. history in comparison with other students in the country.
- The assessment will indicate whether students are able to follow the appropriate steps to determine the volume of an object placed in water.

Often, interpretations involve a *construct,* an abstract conception of a trait or characteristic, such as intelligence, self-esteem, attitudes, reasoning ability, anxiety, and values. With constructs, the specific intended meaning must be identified. For example, attitudes may consist of feelings and/or perceptions of importance. To make a proper interpretation, the user needs to know whether a specific attitude survey measured feelings or perceptions of importance. Here are some examples of interpretations related to constructs:

- The assessment will indicate the extent to which students are motivated to learn.
- The assessment will indicate the climate of Mr. Tate's fifth-grade classroom.
- The assessment will identify the students with the lowest self-esteem.

Once the intended claim, interpretation, or inference is determined, the user gathers evidence to support the validity of the claim. The accumulated evidence is what establishes validity. When examining the types of evidence that can be used, it is helpful, I think, to keep in mind that much of the fairly technical language and many of the concepts and approaches to validity were developed for large-scale standardized testing, not for classroom assessment. The specific categories I'll be using to present different types of evidence are based on standards for large-scale and psychological assessments. Although the same categories of evidence can be used for both large-scale and classroom assessments, teachers typically use much less formal applications in the classroom. Whether the evidence is systematic and statistical or informal, the key to validity is that the evidence is appropriate for the type of inference that is made.

I'd like to make one more point before moving on to different sources of validity evidence. An important assumption when making an inference about what a student knows, understands, and can do is that the student tried as much as possible to do well on the test. The motivation, effort, persistence, and seriousness that students bring to the testing situation all contribute to the scores. If we, as teachers or administrators, are not certain about these factors, then our inferences may well be invalid. Take the situation of a state competency exam that is used for school accreditation but has no implications for individual students. How seriously would students take the test, especially if the students are in high school? If they don't try hard, interpreting low scores to mean that the students do not know the content well would be invalid. Or consider a measure of student attitudes. How sure can we be that students are not faking their responses? Although we hope that serious student engagement will be evident in our assessments, we need to examine this element.

Sources of Validity Evidence

Table 2.2 summarizes five types of evidence that can be used to evaluate the legitimacy of a validity claim. These are not types of validity (remember, validity is a singular concept). Different sources of evidence can, and often should, be used to support the same inference. The key is matching the right types of evidence with the intended inferences and uses.

Evidence Based on Test Content or Constructs

One important feature of most types of assessment is that it is difficult, if not impossible, to test students on everything they are taught or everything they have learned. Typically, an identified *domain* represents the nature of what it is that we want to make an inference about. The domain, or universe, consists of all the knowledge, skills, or constructs of interest. What we do is assess a *sample* from the larger domain. Evidence based on test content (also referred to as content-related evidence or content validity) and constructs includes logical and empirical analyses of how well the sample in the assessment that is administered is representative of the larger domain.

For example, suppose a fifth-grade teacher is giving a unit test on insects, and the teacher intends to use the scores to show how much each student knows about everything that has been taught during the 6-week unit. Can you imagine how long the test would need to be to cover every fact, concept, and principle that students had been taught? The teacher must make some decisions to sample content from the entire domain and then use the scores on the sample items to make inferences about how much each student knows as

Table 2.2 Summary of Sources of Evidence

Evidence Based On	Description
Test content or construct	Extent to which the assessment items represent a larger domain of interest or construct
Relations to other variables	High correlations with other measures of the same variable or criterion measures and low correlations with measures of related but different variables
Internal structure	Extent to which items measuring the same thing are correlated
Response processes and results	Consistency between hypothesized processes used and expected results with actual processes used and results
Consequences	Extent to which intended and unintended consequences of the assessment are appropriate and desired

defined in the larger domain. For example, if a student scores 75% correct on the test, the teacher infers that the student knows 75% of the content in the entire unit. How do you know if the teacher's decisions about the content to include in the test are such that the inference about the entire domain, which is made on the basis of the sample test items, is accurate? Here validity becomes a matter of professional judgment. In classroom assessment, the teacher usually makes a judgment about whether the sample is representative of the larger domain. This judgment process can be superficial or systematic. In a superficial review, the teacher makes the judgment in haste on the basis of appearance only. This is sometimes referred to as *face* validity. Face validity means that on a superficial review of the test, the content appears to be representative of the larger domain. Although we clearly want to avoid face *in*validity, more structured and systematic evidence is desirable.

Evidence Based on Test Content

In large-scale educational achievement testing, evidence based on test content begins with a detailed description of the content domain. Once the content domain is defined, items are developed and included in the test to represent the domain. These specifications, called *test blueprints* or *tables of specification,* will show the user and interpreter of the test the extent to which different content areas have been covered. An example of a test blueprint for the Virginia state testing program is illustrated in Table 2.3. In this example,

Table 2.3 Example of Large-Scale Third-Grade Science Test Blueprint

Reporting Categories	No. of Items	Kindergarten SOLs	Grade 1 SOLs	Grade 2 SOLs	Grade 3 SOLs
Scientific investigation	10	K.1a-j K.2a-c	1.1a-g	2.1a-h	3.1a-k
Force, motion, energy, and matter	10	K.3a, b K.4a-e K.5a-c	1.2a-d 1.3a-c	2.2a, b 2.3a, b	3.2a-c 3.3a-c
Life processes and living systems*	10	K.6a-c	1.4a-c 1.5a-c	2.4a, b 2.5a, b 2.7a 2.8a-c	3.4a, b 3.5a-c 3.6a-c 3.10a
Earth/space systems and cycles*	10	K.7a, b K.8a-d K.9a, b K.10a-c	1.6a, b 1.7a-c 1.8a-d	2.6a, b 2.7b	3.7a-d 3.8a, b 3.9a-c 3.10b-d 3.11a-e

SOLs excluded from this test: No SOLs are excluded.

Total number of operational items:	40
*Field-test items:	10
Total number of items:	50

NOTE: SOLs stands for Standards of Learning. Numbers and letters in the table refer to specific standards. Reporting categories are test subscales. This test includes SOL for four grade levels.

state "Standards of Learning" (SOL) were used to indicate the content and skills to be covered on the tests. To establish strong evidence based on content, experts in the subject areas reviewed the tests and made systematic judgments about whether the items represented the content. These experts also made judgments about whether the percentage of items in different areas was appropriate and whether some areas that would be important were not on the test. With several individuals making such judgments, the review process is fairly systematic.

In the development of large-scale national standardized tests, the test developers will invest significant resources to be sure that appropriate knowledge and skills are assessed. For commercial test companies, who want their tests to be used in as many schools as possible, this process begins with suggestions from nationally recognized subject matter experts and, more recently, with content standards identified by national associations. Leading textbooks would also be examined to determine the domain of content and skills. Teachers and college professors might be used to indicate the nature of

Table 2.4 Example of Classroom Assessment Test Blueprint

	Cognitive Level of Learning			
Topic Area	*Knowledge*	*Reasoning*	*Application*	*Total*
Types of clouds	5	3	4	12
Types of fronts	5	2	4	11
High and low pressure	6	6	5	17
Wind	7	3	6	16
Total	23	14	19	56

NOTE: The number of items is shown in this blueprint. Percentages of items can also be used to provide an overview of what is emphasized in different areas.

key concepts, ideas, and skills. Following item generation, teachers may be used to examine each item and classify it according to categories of the subject domain and type of cognitive skill being assessed (e.g., recall knowledge or understanding).

For classroom assessment, test blueprints are sometimes used to indicate what will be assessed as well as the nature of the learning that will be represented in the assessment. An example of such a test blueprint is shown in Table 2.4. It is a two-way grid in which items are classified by content area and by the cognitive level of the learning. Although making such a blueprint provides a systematic approach to evidence based on content, constructing one for each assessment may be an imposing task, and many teachers will conclude that in practice, the time it takes to do it outweighs the benefits derived. An alternative is to build a complete set of the learning objectives or targets, showing the number and/or percentage of test devoted to each.

To make judgments about their assessments, teachers need to have a clear understanding of the nature and structure of the discipline that is taught. They need to know what constitutes true understanding and what is most essential to developing appropriate breadth and depth of the discipline. To do this, it is helpful for teachers to discuss with others what constitutes essential understandings and principles and to review assessments to make judgments about whether an assessment, when considered as a whole, reflects these understandings and principles.

Finally, with the popularity of performance assessments, teachers need to extend the essential meaning of validity to how performance is scored. That is, the nature of the scoring criteria needs to reflect important learning objectives. For example, if students are to learn a science skill in which a series of steps needs to be performed, a task that asks students to show their work would help establish a valid inference about whether students have the skill. In addition, to help provide a more valid inference, the scoring of the answers would take into account which steps the students demonstrated and which steps the students did not, giving partial credit where appropriate. If the teacher simply marks each item as correct or incorrect, the total score may not indicate very well what degree of skill the student actually possesses. That is, if items are scored solely as right or wrong, it would be an invalid inference to conclude that the student who missed all the items possesses none of the skills.

Evidence Based on Test Constructs

In a similar way, test users make judgments about the nature of a construct that is being assessed by examining the items to determine if all aspects or components of the construct are represented in the appropriate degree. With constructs, we usually begin with a theoretical definition and rationale, then build the assessment to be consistent with that definition and rationale. This is important because of the abstract nature of construct. That is, there are different ways of conceptualizing a construct, none of which is necessarily better than others. Consider the construct "critical thinking." To examine critical thinking in education, you need a good match between what you want to emphasize in your school and the definition and theory represented in the particular measure you would like to use. Once the theory is consistent, an examination of the items is needed to make a judgment about the representativeness of the items as related to the theoretical rationale.

Suppose a school decided to use a new student self-report instrument that was purportedly designed to identify students who are most at risk to fail and drop out of school. The instrument could be based on a theoretical model of resilience in which various factors contributing to resilience, such as having a hobby and a good relationship with an adult, were assessed. For use in a particular school, teachers would need to review the theoretical rationale and agree that it seemed reasonable for their students, then review the items to determine if the items were consistent with the theoretical rationale and weighted appropriately in the scoring.

Whether the concern is with content or construct evidence to establish validity, it is important in both large-scale and classroom assessment to determine what could be called *instructional* validity, or evidence based on instruction. Instructional validity is concerned with the match between what is taught or what students have the opportunity to learn, and what is assessed. What is the match between what was taught and what was assessed? Have students had an appropriate opportunity to learn what was assessed? These questions are important because they relate directly to many of the inferences to be made. Suppose a national norm-referenced achievement test is used to determine mathematics achievement. If the mathematics content in the test is not matched with what students have been taught, it would be unreasonable to conclude that the low scores mean that the school is not doing a good job. Similarly, it would not be valid to conclude that a school with low scores on a state competency exam is deficient or poor if the instruction provided does not match well with what is on the exam.

For a classroom teacher, this essentially means asking the question, "Were the concepts actually taught, and taught well enough, so that students can perform well and demonstrate their understanding?" Often, this type of judgment is made just before an assessment is written in final form and administered because the answer can be known only after instruction has occurred. Although teachers may begin with an instructional plan, and even have an assessment instrument that is already prepared, not until most of the instruction is completed can the teacher determine the match between what has been taught and emphasized and what is on the test. In making this determination, the teacher, one hopes, will also be able to conclude that student performance is due to learning and not to other factors such as the format of the assessment (e.g., some students are better with multiple-choice), gender, social desirability (e.g., pleasing the teacher when completing an attitude survey), and other influences that would lessen the validity.

Evidence Based on Relations to Other Variables

A second way to ensure appropriate inferences from assessment results is to have evidence that the scores are related to other variables in significant and predictable ways. There are two types of such evidence, one based on how a measure is related to other, external measures (test-criterion relationships) and one based on obtaining a pattern of relationships (convergent and discriminant evidence). Most of my emphasis will be on the first type. But before we consider these types of evidence, let's review the meaning of measures of relationship and two statistical concepts that are used in describing relationships—scatterplot and correlation.

Measures of Relationship

Measures of relationship are used to indicate, for a group of examinees, the degree to which two scores from different measures are related, that is, whether scores from one assessment are associated with, or predict, scores from another assessment. Suppose Ms. Lopez has a small class of students and is interested in the relationship between her classroom semester geometry test and a standardized geometry test of the same content. She gives both tests to her students and reports scores summarized in Table 2.5. When these scores are rank ordered and compared, it is evident that there is some degree of relationship because students who obtained a high score on the classroom semester test also obtained a high score on the standardized test. In other words, in a rough sense, scores from one test can predict approximate scores on the other test. If there were no relationship, there would be no pattern or

Table 2.5 Classroom Exam Scores and Standardized Test Scores

Student	Semester Exam Score	Standardized Test Score	Semester Exam Rank	Standardized Test Rank
1. Molly	97	93	1	3
2. Ted	95	95	2	1
3. Dan	94	94	3	2
4. Cheryl	90	89	4	6
5. Ryann	88	91	5	4
6. Jon	86	90	6	5
7. Hannah	85	84	7	8
8. Tyron	82	85	8	7
9. Jim	79	82	9	10
10. Jan	78	79	10	12
11. Bill	77	83	11	9
12. Maria	75	77	12	13
13. Frank	72	71	13	15
14. Carl	71	80	14	11
15. Tom	68	73	15	14

prediction. Students with high scores on the semester test might have low standardized scores, and those obtaining low semester exam scores might have high standardized scores.

Scatterplots

Another way to represent the nature of the relationship is by forming a visual array of the intersections of the students' scores on the two tests. This is called a *scatterplot* or *scattergram*. It is essentially a graphic representation of the relationship. As illustrated in Figure 2.2, the ranges of possible scores on each test are represented on each axis of the graph, from low to high, and the points at which each student's scores intersect are placed in the graph. This results in one point for each student. When the plotting is completed for all students, a pattern is formed that provides a general indication of the strength and direction of the relationship. The direction of the pattern indicates whether the relationship is positive, negative (or inverse), or whether there is curvilinear, or no relationship. We are concerned here with positive relationships, illustrated in Figure 2.2. A relationship is positive if scores on one test increase as scores on the other test increase. No relationship is indicated when the points are scattered with no pattern at all. The strength of the relationship is shown by the degree to which the points cluster together around an imaginary line down the middle of the pattern. The more tightly clustered the points, the stronger the relationship.

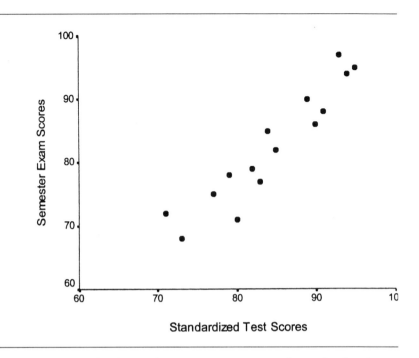

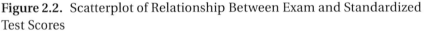

Figure 2.2. Scatterplot of Relationship Between Exam and Standardized
Test Scores

Correlation Coefficient

A *correlation coefficient* is a number between -1 and +1 that is calculated to
represent the direction and strength of the relationship. A high positive value
(e.g., .90, .83) indicates a strong positive relationship, whereas a low positive
value (e.g., .20, .13) indicates a weak positive relationship. A high negative
value (e.g., -.88, -.94) indicates a strong negative relationship, whereas a low
negative value (e.g., -.22, -.10) indicates a weak negative relationship. For the
scores reported in Table 2.5 and illustrated in Figure 2.2, the calculated correlation coefficient is .94. Correlation coefficients are used extensively in standardized testing for reporting evidence of relationships but are seldom used
with classroom assessments. Chapter 5 looks more closely at scatterplots and
correlation, but for now, this is a sufficient explanation to consider how validity evidence is demonstrated through relationships.

Test-Criterion Relationships

One type of relationship occurs when a set of scores is correlated to another
measure of the same content or construct or to some behavior or performance. This other measure, behavior, or performance is usually called a *crite-*

rion measure. A correlation coefficient is calculated as a measure of the relationship and may be called the *validity coefficient*. Traditionally, there are two types of test-criterion relationships: *concurrent criterion-related* and *predictive criterion-related*. A concurrent coefficient indicates a relationship between two measures that are given at about the same time. A concurrent coefficient is illustrated with the example of Ms. Lopez's class. A predictive criterion-related coefficient indicates how accurately test data can predict scores from a criterion measure that are gathered at a later time.

Predictive criterion-related evidence is used extensively in education, even if not labeled as such, because predictive inferences are valuable in selecting students for special programs and directing students to appropriate instructional interventions. Teachers constantly make informal predictions of student learning, based on their observations of student work or answers to questions. With experience, teachers learn that certain types of behavior and student responses will be correlated to how well students can do on tests. Once this relationship is established, it can be used to help future students obtain the assistance they need to succeed.

Predictive criterion-related correlation coefficients are used in standardized testing in a more formal way. Standardized aptitude tests are the best example. The purpose of these tests is to predict future performance on the criterion measure. First, students are administered the aptitude test. After a time has elapsed, the students are measured on the criterion that the test is supposed to predict. For example, the Scholastic Assessment Test (SAT) is an aptitude test in which the criterion is how well students perform in college. The correlation of students' scores from the SAT and grades in college indicates the extent of the predictive evidence. Several factors affect the magnitude of the correlation, including the length of time between the predictor and the criterion (as the time between the measures increases, the correlation decreases), the degree of error in the predictor and criterion measure (more error lowers the correlation), and the extent to which the criterion measure is influenced by factors that are not accounted for in the predictor measure.

The effect of the many influences on the criterion measure is usually the biggest culprit in establishing predictive evidence. Consider the use of grades obtained in college as a criterion measure for the SAT. Think for a moment about all the factors that affect student grades. Motivation, study skills, peer groups, work, family, effort, goals, and interpersonal skills are all important in determining grades, in addition to academic aptitude as measured by the SAT. Actually, student grades in high school are better predictors of college grades than any aptitude test because they tend to account for more factors. On the other hand, predictors that are almost the same as criterion measures (e.g, aptitude tests given at different ages) will result in a high correlation.

Given these influences, it is not surprising that the correlations typically reported as evidence based on predictive criterion-related relationships are moderate (e.g., .50 to .60). This means that the predictor measure can provide some degree of prediction, but it will be far from perfect. This is one reason why important placement decisions should never be made solely on the basis of a single test score. For instance, requiring students to take remedial summer school if they fail to achieve a designated "cut score" on a measure that purportedly predicts how well students will perform the following year is problematic because many factors contribute to student performance. The result achieved on the predictor test can represent only a part of the prediction.

Convergent and Discriminant Evidence

Strong evidence for validity is demonstrated when certain patterns of correlations are reported for two or more measures or instruments. *Convergent* evidence is obtained when scores from one instrument correlate highly with scores from another measure of the same trait or performance (similar to concurrent criterion-related evidence). *Discriminant* evidence exists when scores from one instrument correlate poorly with scores from another measure of something different. When convergent correlations are high and the discriminant correlations are low, the pattern suggests strong evidence. For example, scores from a measure of self-concept would be expected to correlate highly with scores from a different but similar measure of self-concept but to show low correlation with related but different traits such as anxiety and motivation. The discriminant pattern can also be found by examining the subscales within a single instrument. For self-concept, for example, there are often different subscales (academic, social, and physical). Strong evidence for validity would exist if the subscales are not too highly correlated with each other.

Convergent and discriminant evidence is commonly gathered in developing psychological instruments that assess constructs such as self-concept, personality, attitudes, values, interests, and beliefs. In the classroom, teachers can apply the logic of this type of evidence by taking note of the consistency of student performance on different measures of the same knowledge or skill (convergent) and by seeing if there is less correlation with assessments of different knowledge or skills (discriminant). This is useful in identifying specific areas that need attention. For example, a teacher might use the following logic as evidence that an inference about a student's comprehension skills is valid: "Sam is able to read all types of different reading passages well in class and on standardized tests (convergent evidence) but doesn't always demonstrate a clear understanding of what he reads (discriminant evidence)." The inference is that Sam needs further instruction in comprehension. This conclusion would be less valid if based only on comprehension scores because there would be no evidence that the measure of comprehension was different from reading ability.

Evidence Based on Internal Structure

Large-scale and psychological assessments are usually designed so that several items are used to measure each separate trait or important reporting category. The item clusters are identified by how a construct is defined or by identified categories. For example, a measure of classroom climate would have several similar items that indicate a given theoretical dimension of climate, such as friendship or cohesiveness. If the items focusing on friendship are strongly related to each other and, at the same time, related less to items measuring other components, then there is good evidence based on internal structure. On the other hand, if the friendship items correlate highly with cohesion or goal orientation, or some other dimensions, then the evidence is weak, meaning that it may not be appropriate to report friendship as a separate aspect of classroom climate. Thus, evidence based on internal structure is provided when the relationships among items and parts of the instrument are empirically consistent with the construct, theory, or intended use of the scores.

In the classroom, this type of evidence is typically used in criterion-referenced testing, albeit informally. Teachers use the combined results of several items that cover the same skill, concept, principle, or application. It is recommended that students need to answer a minimum of six to eight selected-response items to obtain sufficient consistency to conclude from the results that the students do or do not understand.

To illustrate, suppose a math teacher is constructing a unit geometry test. One of the skills to be assessed is the ability to determine the area of circles and cylinders. To obtain good evidence based on internal structure, the test needs to have several items that assess the ability of the students to determine area of circles and several items focused on cylinders. It wouldn't make much sense to give a two-item test—one item on circles and one on cylinders. Rather, several items for each are needed, and consistency in responses would provide good evidence for the validity of the inference that students do or do not know how to find the area of circles and cylinders.

Evidence Based on Response Processes and Results

To make inferences about thinking processes and skills, it is important from a validity standpoint to be able to check that the targeted processes or skills are being engaged in. For example, in teaching the process of writing, teachers need evidence that students are using the appropriate reasoning skills, rather than rote application of an algorithm. Or, if measuring self-concept, teachers don't want students answering questions based on how they want to be perceived rather than how they view themselves. This type of evidence goes beyond a given answer and explores what was behind it—what type of thinking led to the result. For example, students can be asked about their performance strategies and responses to specific items.

Evidence based on response processes is routinely gathered by math teachers who have students "show their work" and who give feedback based not only on the correct answer but also on understanding the procedure for arriving at the answer. Social studies teachers who ask students to explain their answers obtain this type of evidence because they are exploring the reasoning and logic that were used. Many of the new forms of assessment, including performance and portfolio assessment, are ideally suited to gathering this type of evidence because these assessments usually require a depth of student responses that allows adequate evaluation of the strategies employed and because thinking skills are important learning targets.

Evidence based on the results obtained from assessments is helpful when the assessments conform to results that would be hypothesized by theory or logic. One approach is to implement an *intervention study*. In this type of study, a group of students is assessed before and after instruction that is targeted to a specific outcome (e.g., knowledge, skill, or performance). If scores improve significantly after the intervention, then there is validity evidence that the inference about how students have changed is accurate. For example, a social studies competency exam could be developed to identify students who had inadequate knowledge to pass the test. If the identified students are given an intensive tutoring program that focuses specifically on the knowledge needed to pass the exam, and they subsequently do pass it, then there is evidence to support the validity of the claim that students possess the knowledge needed to demonstrate adequate performance.

Another approach examines how different populations that are expected to differ on the knowledge or skills being assessed actually perform. Suppose a new computer technology test is developed. Three groups of students are identified: those with computers in the home and school, those with computers only at school, and those without computers in the home or school. The hypothesis is that scores on the computer technology test will vary, depending on the experiences of each student. Those with the most access to computers are expected to obtain the highest score, and those with least experience, to obtain the lowest. If the test scores comparing the groups are consistent with this prediction, that is evidence that the scores accurately represent computer technology skills and not other skills or competencies.

The logic of comparing different populations can easily be extended into the classroom. When teachers obtain test scores of their students that are inconsistent with other indicators of student performance, such as work done in class, homework, and responses to questions, they appropriately question the validity of the inference from the test scores. It's like asking, "Marie has given every indication in class that she really knows the plot and main characters in the book, but on the test she didn't do well. Is her test score an accurate (valid) indicator of her actual knowledge?" At the least, a teacher asking this question has a healthy skepticism toward test scores that are inconsistent with other performance indicators. It would also be appropriate to review the test, as well as the individual circumstances of the student, to determine if anything unintended is influencing the results.

Evidence Based on the Consequences of Assessments

In recent years, there has been considerable discussion among testing experts about whether the overall judgment of validity of uses and interpretations should include a consideration of the possible *consequences* of using the assessments (Messick, 1989, 1995; Popham, 1997; Shepard, 1997). Consequences could be both planned and unintended. For example, a desirable consequence of using essay questions may be that students learn the content with more depth of understanding than if they prepare for a multiple-choice test. For many tests, the implicit purpose is to have predetermined consequences, such as a placement test to determine which level of a foreign language the student should take, a high school graduation test to determine if a student is eligible to obtain a graduation certificate, end-of-year course tests to screen students for summer school, and tests with children with special needs to determine treatment plans and Individual Educational Plans (IEPs). Clearly, in all these cases, the use of the assessment involves important consequences.

The evidence based on consequences examines the intended effects to see if what was hoped for actually occurs. That is, does the student given a foreign language placement test do better than a student who obtained a similar score but took a different level? Do students who are required, on the basis of the placement test, to take a remedial course do better than students who do not take the remedial course? Do students who are "forced" to attend summer school improve in their performance? Do the consequences of having a specific IEP suggest that the student is learning more, is more motivated, and is happier? In each of these cases, it is possible to collect evidence on the effect to evaluate the validity of the use of the scores.

On a more informal level, teachers use the concept of consequential validity continuously. For example, teachers may assess student understanding during instruction with some questions and use the results of the "assessment" to form small groups of students. The consequence is forming the small group of students, and the evidence comes in when the performance of the students is examined. If student performance is maximized, then there is evidence that the use of the informal assessment was valid. Or a teacher may decide, on the basis of informal assessment, that the entire class needs remediation before moving on in the textbook. The consequence was doing the remediation. The evidence is whether the remediation helped.

The issue of evidence based on consequences takes on a different perspective when considering broader effects, social consequences, and usually negative, unintended effects. The current trend toward more and more "high-stakes" testing, in which large-scale assessments are used to deny grade promotion, high school graduation, and school accreditation, may result in several negative outcomes in the school, such as a narrowing of the curriculum so that it focuses on only the knowledge and skills measured. Important subjects that are not tested may be ignored. Drill-and-practice instructional activities may be used in excess to ensure that students score well, especially if the test emphasizes knowledge as opposed to reasoning. Suppose teachers become less creative and less spontaneous in response to high-stakes student testing. Will teachers change their classroom assessments to match the format used in a high-stakes test? If so, is this desirable? What is the long-term effect?

At the classroom level, student motivation and learning processes are often influenced by the nature of the assessment. A consequence of heavy use of objective items is to encourage students to learn for recognition, whereas essay items motivate students to learn in a way that stresses the organization of information, principles, and application. An important effect of essay items is to engage students in reasoning skills, something that is much more difficult with objective items.

The issue of consequences of the assessment is particularly important to newer forms of assessment such as authentic assessment, portfolio assessment, and performance assessment. These types of assessments are designed to help students learn that often more than one answer can be correct, that learning can be connected to life in general, that scoring criteria and examples are understood before learning, and that learning involves appropriate opportunities to get feedback and refine performances. The desirability of these effects and their grounding in recent constructivist learning theories are the major reasons why these forms of assessment are becoming so popular.

Suggestions for Enhancing
Classroom Assessment Validity

In large-scale testing, there are established procedures for obtaining correlation coefficients as validity evidence. In classroom assessments, however, teachers must rely largely on nonstatistical procedures to establish the validity of their uses and inferences. Here is a list of suggestions to classroom teachers for enhancing validity:

- Determine if different ways of assessing the same thing give similar results.

- Ask other teachers to review your assessment for clarity and purpose.

- Make sure to sample the performance or behavior several times. Don't rely on a single measure.

- Prepare a blueprint, and, prior to testing, share it with your students.

- Ask other teachers to judge the match between the assessment and learning objectives.

- Compare one group of students who should obtain high scores with students of another group who should obtain low scores.

- Compare scores obtained before instruction with scores obtained after instruction.

- Compare predicted, intended consequences with actual consequences.

- Use different methods to measure the same learning objective.

Validity lies at the heart of teacher decision making by establishing guidelines and procedures for determining the quality of the decisions. Validity is also critical to the appropriate use of standardized, large-scale assessment results. The next chapter shows how another characteristic of assessment, reliability, is a necessary but not sufficient aspect of scores for making reasonable validity claims.

CHAPTER

Reliability

Like validity, the term *reliability* describes an essential characteristic of high-quality assessment. Indeed, the assessment process must provide reliable scores as a necessary condition for validity. Also like validity, reliability is a conclusion based on evidence that is gathered in a variety of ways, and there are clear differences between reliability for classroom assessments and reliability for large-scale assessments.

What Is Reliability?

Reliability can be defined as the extent to which assessment scores are dependable and consistent. That is, reliability is a way to assess the consistency of the scores, whether the same or nearly the same scores are obtained at different times or under different circumstances. Notice that this definition stresses the consistency of *scores*, not tests or other instruments. This point is important because reliability, like validity, is a judgment about the scores obtained from a specific instance in which students were required to respond to questions. The scores, not the test, are reliable.

The emphasis on the reliability of scores, and not of tests themselves, is critical to a complete understanding of reliability. Reliability is not a test characteristic that accompanies the test wherever and whenever it is given because a score that is obtained is influenced by many more factors than the nature or quality of the test. Consequently, to understand the results, you must also understand the factors that may affect the scores. So, although you may hear or read something about "the reliability of the *test*," remember that it really refers to the reliability of the *scores*.

Table 3.1 illustrates the concept of reliability with two sets of scores. Two 20-question quizzes are used to assess second graders' addition and subtraction skills at different times. The same addition and subtraction test is used each time. If the results are reliable, there will be a high degree of consistency between the two sets of scores that measure either addition or subtraction. In

Table 3.1 Student Performance on Quizzes (Number Correct) to Illustrate Reliability

Student	Addition		Subtraction	
	Quiz 1	*Quiz 2*	*Quiz 1*	*Quiz 2*
Felix	15	16	12	18
Ryan	12	13	19	11
Rob	19	18	20	14
Deon	18	18	13	19
Mary	10	11	9	20

this example, the addition scores are consistent, pretty much the same from one time to the next time, which indicates high reliability. In contrast, there is little consistency in the results obtained for the subtraction quiz. What does this mean? Because the goal is to have a good estimate of the students' level of skills, the consistency of the scores on the addition quiz allows the test user to make reasonable inferences (e.g., Deon has much stronger addition skills than does Mary). The inconsistent results on the subtraction quizzes, however, mean that these scores should not be used to make inferences about the subtraction skills of the students. More subtraction assessments that yield dependable results would be needed to establish reliability.

Here is another example to illustrate the meaning of reliability. Think about the difference between a measure of self-concept and a measure of the time taken to complete a sailboat race (number of hours, minutes, and seconds). The measure of self-concept will have relatively low consistency because so many factors affect how an individual responds to questions about self-concept, such as the person's mood that day, recent experiences, time of day, heat in the room, degree of fatigue, what the person was told about the survey, and so on. The measure of time, on the other hand, provides a reliable result—a precise, dependable indication of time with little possible error. Even with a measure of time, however, there is some degree of error, such as the dependability of the watch and the ability of the timekeeper to press stop or start appropriately. The way of thinking about possible sources of error provides the foundation for estimating reliability.

Reliability and validity are easily confused because both are concerned with scores and not instruments and because the language seems similar (valid inferences are accurate; reliable scores are dependable). Think of the difference in this way: Reliability addresses whether scores are consistent, whereas validity concerns the nature and meaning of the scores. For example, a measure of the circumference of each student's wrist will provide a reliable result, but it would be absurd to use the scores to indicate reading ability. Like-

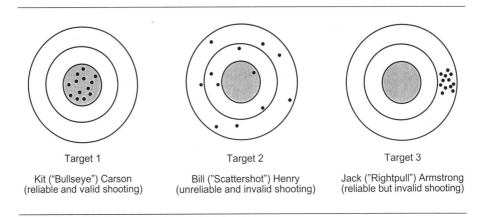

Figure 3.1. Validity and Reliability

SOURCE: From *Measurement and Assessment in Teaching: Student Exercise Manual*, p. 48, by R. L. Linn and N. E. Gronlund. Copyright © 1995. Reprinted by permission of Prentice-Hall, Inc., Upper Saddle River, NJ.

wise, a multiple-choice computer literacy test may provide reliable scores (students get about the same score each time they take the test), but it may not be valid to infer that the students who obtain high scores have stronger computer application skills than students who obtain low scores. Figure 3.1 provides an additional illustration of the relationship between validity and reliability. Think of the target as a learning objective, with the center being the essence of what needs to be assessed. It shows how a measure can be highly reliable (target 3) yet at the same time invalid.

How Is Reliability Determined?

Reliability is determined by estimating the amount of error that accompanies the obtained score. If there is little error, then the reliability is high or strong. If there is much error, the reliability is low or weak. How, then, do we go about estimating the degree of error? It is helpful to consider two major sources of error, those rooted in the students (called internal) and those that are external to the students. Internal factors include those that can vary from one time to another or from one situation to another but reside within the person. For instance, each of us knows how our moods can change and affect our performance. We can have the same knowledge but test poorly on one day because we are sick and score high another day, in part, because we feel sharp. External factors include influences that are outside the person, such as differences among testing sites regarding the distractions students must put up with, test question ambiguity, random error, and differences attributed to scorer subjectivity.

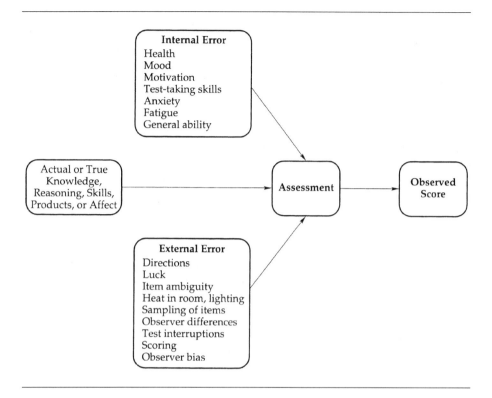

Figure 3.2. Sources of Error in Assessment

SOURCE: From *Classroom Assessment: Principles and Practice for Effective Instruction* (2nd ed.), by J. H. McMillan, in press, Boston: Allyn & Bacon. Copyright © by Allyn & Bacon, Incorporated. Used with permission.

Internal and external sources of error are illustrated in Figure 3.2, which shows how they are combined to influence the observed score or result. Think about three sources of influence that determine the observed score: the actual knowledge or skill of the student, internal factors, and external factors.

It would be nice if assessment results were dependent only on students' knowledge or skill, but that simply doesn't happen with a single test or performance. *There is always some degree of internal and/or external error contributing to the observed score.* Reliability helps estimate the amount of internal and external error, but most traditional reliability procedures *underestimate the actual amount of error.* In other words, there is typically more error than may be reported by reliability data. This is especially true for newer forms of assessment that use scorer judgments to make ratings of performance. The potency of any single error factor depends on the testing situation, nature of the assessment, scoring, and how scores are interpreted. A particular factor, such as conditions of the room, can have a major impact on scores in one assessment but have a minor influence on another assessment.

Reliability is determined by estimating the influence of various sources of error. In large-scale testing, the process is formalized by calculating correlations and reporting the correlations as reliability coefficients. In classroom assessment, there is rarely any statistical estimate of reliability, although software programs make this quite easy. Rather, in classrooms, teachers informally notice some sources of error and take them into account in interpreting results. For example, if Ms. Lopez knows that Susan is distracted by a family problem and simply doesn't concentrate on the test, she can conclude that Susan's low score is heavily influenced by this external factor. In other words, the observed score has considerable error. The reliability of the assessment *for Susan* is weak. It could be strong for other students.

The ideal way to obtain an estimate of the influence of most sources of error, for most assessments, is to give the assessment and then repeat it with a different form of the assessment. But how often is this possible? It is not realistic to expect teachers to create equal forms and repeat the same assessment process over again just to determine degree of error. But it is worthwhile for teachers to keep this ideal in mind to be reminded of the various sources of error. A more practical approach to thinking about error is to consider two major dimensions of consistency, time and content. If an assessment is given once with one form, then the only evidence that can be obtained is restricted to knowledge of that particular situation and the way items within the assessment are related. In large-scale and psychological assessments, this is called *internal consistency*. Looking at consistency through time (same test given twice) uses logic based on the *stability* of the assessment. Two forms of a test can be given at about the same time (*equivalence*), or, as suggested as the most complete way to assess error, different test forms can be given at different times (*stability and equivalence*). These two dimensions of reliability and types of coefficients are summarized in Figure 3.3. The following sections consider in further detail the first three approaches to estimating reliability from the perspective of both large-scale and classroom assessments, as well as scorer or rater consistency.

Sources of Reliability Evidence

Evidence Based on Stability

A stability estimate of reliability refers to consistency through time. The stability of scores is estimated by administering an assessment to a group of individuals, waiting for a specified time (typically a week or more), and then re-administering the same assessment to the same group of individuals. The correlation between the two sets of scores is then calculated to obtain a statis-

	CONTENT (Form)	
	Same	Different
First Administration	Internal Consistency	Equivalence
Second Administration	Stability	Equivalence and Stability

TIME

Figure 3.3. Relationship of Time and Content to Different Types of Reliability

SOURCE: Adapted from *Applied Educational Assessment,* 1st edition, by D. A. Payne. Copyright © 1997. Reprinted with permission of Wadsworth Publishing, a division of Thomson Learning. Fax 800 730-2215.

tical indication of the reliability. This type of estimate is also called *test-retest* reliability. The example of test scores in Table 3.1 is an example of two informal stability estimates. If the performance is about the same on the second test as it was on the first test, as was true for addition in Table 3.1, then the reliability is high. But if the results look like those for the subtraction tests in Table 3.1, the stability and reliability of the scores are both low.

Stability estimates constitute good evidence for reliability when the trait or performance that is assessed is not expected to change during the time span between the assessments. For this reason, stability estimates are not typically used for psychological assessments that measure traits that are expected to change through time, such as mood and perception. Also, many psychological instruments (as well as some measures of achievement) are *reactive:* Persons taking the assessment once may change simply because of the experience of taking it. With achievement tests, students may change their performance because of practice and memory. In measuring abilities, such as reading comprehension, change would be hoped for during the long term, but during a short time span, the scores would be expected to be stable. Because aptitude test scores are used to make inferences about future behavior or performance, stability evidence needs to be collected. A readiness test that measures aptitudes and abilities with the purpose of predicting success is an example. These scores would not be useful if there wasn't some assurance that the aptitudes and abilities are stable between the time tested and time of placement.

Stability estimates are often low because of the number of factors that can affect the scores, some of which I have already discussed. One way to think about it is to examine the internal and external sources of error in Figure 3.2 and see how these could vary from one instance to another. Time becomes a critical factor that influences the correlation. There is an inverse relationship between the time span between the two administration times and the strength of the correlation. That is, as the time interval increases, the correlation decreases.

In general, stability estimates in the form of correlation coefficients will not be used in classroom assessment. But teachers will benefit from using the logic of stability in evaluating student work. When performances should be stable, an informal review of the results, by comparing scores or ranks, will provide some evidence of reliability. Another approach is for teachers to examine the consistency of decisions made about students through time. For example, a teacher may use an assessment to place students in cooperative groups. On the basis of the test scores, students may be placed into one of three groups—high, medium, and low. From a stability standpoint for reliability, the teacher could use the same assessment again and determine the percentage of students classified the same way on both assessments. Here the focus is not on the specific scores but on the decision. If most or even many of the students are classified differently the second time, then the assessment would not be reliable. As we will see, decision-oriented evidence also plays a major role in providing reliability data for criterion-referenced assessments.

Evidence Based on Equivalent Forms

An estimate of equivalence is obtained by administering two forms of the same assessment to a group of students and correlating the scores. This type of evidence may be called *alternate* or *parallel form* reliability. The approach is to generate two forms of an assessment that are equal in what is being measured. If the two forms are given at approximately the same time (same day or week), then an estimate of only equivalence is obtained. If there is a significant time delay between the administrations, then a stability feature is added, providing an estimate of equivalence *and* stability.

In classroom assessment, teachers rarely use formal equivalence evidence because it would be unusual to have to generate more than a single form of each assessment. But equivalence is a factor if students are offered makeup tests or if teachers want to use different forms in a pretest-posttest research design. The difficulty for teachers is knowing when two forms are "equivalent." On a more informal level, teachers use the logic of equivalent forms when they have different types of assessment of the same skill or content. Often, test scores are only one measure. Quizzes, homework, and class participation are used to obtain additional measures of students' knowledge, understanding, and skill. Research on teacher assessment and grading practices has shown that most teachers use multiple assessments (Cizek, Rachor,

& Fitzgerald, 1996; Frary, Cross, & Weber, 1993; McMillan, 1999a; Stiggins & Conklin, 1992).

Equivalent forms evidence is used extensively in standardized testing and high-stakes testing in which students need to pass tests to advance in grade or graduate from high school. Several forms of the same test are needed to allow retakes and makeup testing. If tests are used in this way, evidence based on equivalence is essential. A relatively new procedure, called *item response theory*, is often used with standardized tests to establish reliable scores on tests that invariably differ somewhat with respect to difficulty.

Evidence Based on Internal Consistency

Internal consistency evidence is based on the degree of homogeneity of the items that measure the same trait in an assessment. Unlike for stability and equivalence, only a single administration of an assessment is needed. The logic is that if many items measure the same thing, scores based on these items should be correlated with each other. For example, a teacher would expect a student who has clearly mastered knowledge of the parts of a flower to get most or all items correct on a 10-question test. In contrast, a student who knew nothing about the parts of flowers would be expected to get most of or all of the 10 items wrong. In other words, internal consistency estimates how well items within an assessment are functioning in a consistent manner.

There are three common types of internal consistency estimates: *split-half, Kuder-Richardson,* and *coefficient alpha.* In the split-half method, the test items are typically divided into "equal" halves by whether the items are even numbered or odd numbered; then each half is scored separately for each student. The total scores for each of the halves are correlated to provide a reliability coefficient. This approach works fine for tests that have 10 or more items measuring the same trait. If the assessment has a more restricted number of items, it is best to match items that seem to be closest to form the halves, rather than use the odd-even strategy. Because only half the test items are used to calculate the correlation, the *Spearman-Brown* formula is used to estimate the correlation for the entire test.

The Kuder-Richardson formulas (KR 20, KR 21) are used for tests in which each item is scored dichotomously (e.g., right or wrong). You can think of the KR approaches as the average of correlating the totals from all possible halves. This avoids the problem of having to determine how to separate the scores to obtain equal halves. When assessments are scored using a scale that has more than two levels, such as what is commonly found in attitude surveys (e.g., using a scale such as strongly agree, agree, disagree, strongly disagree), coefficient alpha is used to generate a reliability coefficient.

Because internal consistency evidence can be obtained by giving an assessment once to one group of students, its use has become widespread. From a practical standpoint, internal consistency evidence is easy to establish. There is no need to develop a second form, nor is it necessary to give the assessment more than once. There are some limitations, however. One, there needs to be a sufficient number of items. The rule of thumb is that at least five items are needed to measure each separate trait or skill. Two, it is not appropriate to use internal consistency for assessments that have a time limit that makes it difficult for many students to complete the test (speeded tests). This is common in standardized testing and results in an inflated correlation coefficient. Because there is usually sufficient time for students to be able to complete most classroom assessments, this limitation is not a factor for teachers when interpreting the results of their assessments.

Three, many sources of error related to stability are not included in calculating the correlation. This is an important consideration in classroom tests because teachers want to know that students can demonstrate a skill or can show their understanding *consistently*, that is, from day to day or week to week. We want students to remember what they have learned. If the only estimate we have is internal consistency data, the best we can conclude is that students were able to demonstrate understanding and skill *at that particular time*, with the amount of error calculated mostly on the basis of the quality of the items and procedures for gathering the data. Changes in the person from day to day would not be accounted for. In other words, internal consistency estimates alone will underestimate the actual amount of error that should be considered in interpreting the scores.

Evidence Based on Scorer or Rater Consistency

Whenever student responses need to be judged, rated, or scored, an additional source of error is introduced that may be important. Examples of these types of assessments include grading essays, scoring writing samples, evaluating performance assessments and portfolios, and grading papers and projects. In each case, someone, usually the classroom teacher, has to review and evaluate the work, and in this evaluation process, additional error is introduced. These errors include biases of the scorer; the halo effect (evaluating on the basis of a general impression of the student, e.g., "Sally is a good student; this answer is good"); fatigue; general expectations; and other idiosyncrasies of the scorer.

Two approaches can be used to establish reliability evidence based on scorer or rater consistency: a percentage agreement approach and a correlational approach. The percentage agreement method typically uses simple agreement among two or more raters or agreement within one or more points. It is obtained by asking two or more scorers or raters to judge the same set of student performances. The number of exact matches can be added and then divided by the total number of judgments to get a percentage that indi-

Table 3.2 Portfolio Scores Assigned by Different Teachers

Student	Score	
	Teacher 1	*Teacher 2*
Mehdi	5	5
Suzanne	2	3
Angie	5	5
Daisy	6	6
Reed	4	5
Stephen	2	2
Maike	3	3
Pat	1	2
Robert	5	5
Jon	4	4
Faye	4	4
George	3	5
Kim	6	6
Jim	5	5
Kristin	2	2
Diona	4	4
Joel	1	1
Chuck	3	3
David	2	2
Barney	5	4

cates consistency. Suppose, for example, two teachers independently rate a set of 20 student portfolios on a scale of 1 to 6. The results are summarized in Table 3.2. The number of exact matches is 15, which results in an agreement index of 75%, which is good. This indicates that error attributed to the scorer is not great.

If agreement within one point is used, then 19 of the 20 scores would be used to calculate the percentage, now 95%. It's obvious that if you loosen the criteria for what determines a "match," the percentage agreement is going to go up. How do you know which to use, the exact match or matching within one or possibly more points? The answer depends on a number of factors. The first factor is the nature of the scale or rating. If you use more points on a scale, then it makes sense to use matching within one or more points. For example, if teachers were grading essays and gave each one up to 50 points, it might be reasonable to think of a match as within 5 points. On the other hand, if the judgment is into one of three categories, it would be best to use exact matches. The second factor is the description of various points on the scale and the relative distinction between them. Consider the following scoring rubric for language:

1 Inadequate	2 Minimal	3 Adequate	4 Superior
Grammar and vocabulary very poor	Many grammar mistakes made; simplistic language	Few grammar mistakes; appropriate language	Excellent grammar and language

The degree of error with such a scale will probably be high because the criteria listed are vague, without much degree of specificity or clarity that would allow assigning each example a proper score. In the following scale, the criteria are much more detailed and would lead to a higher percentage of agreement.

1 Inadequate	2 Minimal	3 Adequate	4 Superior
Grammar and vocabulary so poor that most of the message is not understood	Grammar and vocabulary weak but allow understanding. Many grammar mistakes made; simplistic language	Grammar and vocabulary complex with few mistakes; language not overly simplistic	Excellent grammar and vocabulary, with only minor mistakes; language uses a variety of techniques such as humor, imagery, and metaphor

A final factor to consider is the training of the scorers. The expectation is that scorers or raters who are trained will achieve a higher rate of agreement than those not trained. In the training, it is important for the scorers to see many examples of completed products that align with different points on the scale. These examples are sometimes called *anchors* or *benchmarks*. Another consideration is to help scorers understand why a particular judgment is in correct, providing additional practice until a high rate of agreement is achieved.

One limitation of the agreement method is the possibility that two or more raters will agree by chance. This tends to result in agreement percentages that overestimate the consistency. In large-scale assessments, an index referred to as *kappa* is calculated to take account of the probability of making matches by chance. Kappa ranges from -1 (total disagreement) to +1 (total agreement), with a value of 0 indicating chance agreement.

A second method of determining scorer or rater agreement is to calculate a correlation coefficient. With two scorers and a set of scores, such a correlation indicates the strength of agreement between the scorers. For the data from Table 3.2, the correlation is .92, which is very high. In this case, the correlation gives an even stronger indication of reliability, although an agreement index should not be directly compared with a correlation. The limitation with using correlations, in addition to the additional computation, is that the nature of the scale may not meet assumptions that are important in computing correlations. Also, as we will see in Chapter 5, it is always best to include a scatter diagram in interpreting a correlation.

One final caution about scorer or rater agreement: This method does not take into consideration error attributed to the tasks, time, or sampling. Usually, only selected tasks are used, and these tasks are only one way to represent the problem or provide opportunities for students to demonstrate their knowledge or skill. A good example of this is the use of writing prompts when assessing students' writing and language skills. It is clear that some students are better able to respond to certain prompts that others would have difficulty with because of background and interests. So the choice of a prompt is important, as is the choice of the task in performance assessment. If prompts and performance tasks are not selected carefully, they can contribute to a weak generalization to the larger set of prompts or tasks that could be used in the assessment. Consistency through time is not accounted for in scorer or rater agreement. This means that error because of changes in time is not included.

Finally, sampling becomes an important issue because some scoring procedures focus only on easily obtained interscorer agreement and then assume that the process is reliable. Consider this example. Suppose you wanted to assess the readability of several short books and decided to have two raters use the SMOG formula (Simple Measure of Gobbledygook; McLaughlin, 1969). Your strategy is to establish reliability by showing high rater agreement. When using the SMOG formula, the raters count three sets of 10 sentences from the beginning, middle, and end of the book. Then all words with three or more syllables are counted to obtain an index of readability. The scorers count syllables *for the same sentences.* Is it any wonder that there is high rater agreement? With this type of simple task, it would certainly be expected. This may not indicate with precision the reading level of the entire book, however. To do that, a sample of sentences would need to be selected randomly from all sentences. So although the SMOG formula may give "reliable" results from one perspective, inferences concerning the entire book are limited.

Some methods are available for estimating reliability that include several sources of error simultaneously, usually referred to in the context of *generalizability theory.* These methods, however, are beyond the scope of this introduction and are used primarily in research.

Table 3.3 Sources of Evidence in Estimating Reliability

Source of Evidence	Description
Evidence based on stability (test-retest)	Estimates consistency of scores from two administrations of the same assessment to the same individuals with a time interval between the assessments
Evidence based on equivalent forms	Estimates consistency of scores obtained from two forms of the same assessment, given at the same time or with a time interval (equivalence and stability)
Evidence based on internal consistency	Estimates consistency of scores measuring the same trait obtained from a single administration of the assessment
Evidence based on scorer or rater consistency	Estimates consistency of scores by calculating the agreement between two or more scorers or raters of the same performances

Table 3.3 summarizes the four sources of evidence that have been discussed. Keep in mind that even if correlations and percentage agreement are not formally calculated, the logic and type of consistency assessed are unique to each source and should match the nature of the inference you wish to draw from the scores.

Reliability for Criterion-Referenced Interpretations

Much of the early work on reliability was based on tests for which norm-referenced inferences were made. The nature of the tests fit well with obtaining high correlations. But to make criterion-referenced inferences, as is so common in the classroom as well as in new statewide high-stakes testing and standards-based assessment, the nature of the inference as pass/fail, novice/apprentice/expert, or other categorical decisions suggests a different approach to reliability. In addition, by their very nature, assessments used for criterion-referenced interpretations often give a restricted range of scores. In the classroom, for example, most scores are pretty high with only a few low ones. This lowers the size of a correlation coefficient based on these scores. On the other hand, assessments intended for a norm-referenced interpretation provide a set of scores spread out along the possible range of results.

The basic approach for obtaining evidence of reliability for criterion-referenced interpretations is to focus on the decision or classification, rather than the total score, and to examine the consistency of making similar decisions or classifications. For example, if a test is designed to classify students as masters or nonmasters, a "cut" score will be established to make the decision for each student. Without dwelling on the methods of establishing such cut scores (all of which are arbitrary judgments), let's suppose this was done in a reasonable fashion. Consistency is obtained by examining what percentages of the classifications are the same on two administrations of the same test, on different forms of the same test, or on a single administration (similar to internal consistency). Suppose a group of 20 students took the same test twice. On the first administration, 10 were classified as masters, and 10 as nonmasters. Of the 10 classified as masters on the first administration, 8 were classified this way on the second administration. All 10 students initially classified as nonmasters were also classified nonmasters on the second test. So of all the 20 classifications, there were matches with 18. That is, 18 of the 20 students were classified the same way. This can be converted to a percentage—90% in this case.

For those who like formulas for this type of thinking, the following will work when there is a dichotomous classification:

% Consistency = (Number classified master both times + Number classified nonmaster both times) ÷ Total number in the group.

You may be wondering how high the percentage needs to be to conclude that the inference about mastery is reasonably reliable. To answer this question, you need to compare the percentage obtained to what could have been achieved by chance. For example, in a dichotomous classification, if you did the sorting randomly, you would find 50% consistency. So, a result not much beyond 50% indicates poor reliability. At the other extreme, finding 90% consistency suggests that the inference is reliable. When you have more than two classifications, as is the case for many performance and portfolio assessments, the chance percentage is less. Because there is also greater opportunity for misclassification, however, acceptable percentages range from 70% to 85%.

Another element in interpreting the percentage consistently classified concerns the nature of the decision to be made. When criterion-referenced interpretations are used to determine eligibility for graduation or other high-stakes decisions, the standard for reliability needs to be high. Less stringent standards are needed for decisions that do not have important long-term consequences, such as deciding whether to review a given topic for a final exam. For important decisions, there should be several opportunities for students to demonstrate the needed level of competency. A useful way to think about reliability in such situations is to estimate the percentage of students misclassified after several opportunities. The logic in multiple opportunities is that through time, other sources of error can be accounted for. For instance, if a student is not feeling well the first time and fails, the next time provides an opportunity to show what can be done when the student is feeling better.

Factors Influencing Reliability Estimates

Several factors influence the magnitude of reliability estimates that are obtained for large-scale and psychological assessments. Interpretations of reliability coefficients or percentage agreement will be more accurate if these influences are kept in mind.

Spread of Scores

Reliability coefficients are directly related to the degree of spread of the scores that are used in the calculations. Other things being equal, the greater the spread of scores, the higher the reliability. In other words, if the assessment results in a large range of scores, a higher correlation may be obtained. A greater spread results if the group being assessed has a range of scores. This has implications when assessing a group of students who are fairly homogeneous with respect to the trait being assessed (e.g., an honors-level class). Because the students achieve at the same level, there is a low range of scores, and reliability estimates may be low as well. In an extreme case, think about what type of correlation would result if all the students had one of two scores. This lack of heterogeneity will make it difficult to obtain high correlations using traditional reliability indicators. In this type of situation, reliability evidence needs to be gathered from a different pool of students that will show a greater spread of scores.

Number of Assessment Items

The more items of about the same level of difficulty on a test, the higher will be the reliability. This is because a longer assessment with many items does a better job of sampling the trait or behavior. Also, the error associated with specific items has less influence on a longer assessment. Imagine giving students a single mathematics problem to assess their ability to multiply fractions. The scores and resulting inferences about student ability would be highly unreliable. Students would get either a 100 or a 0 on the "test." But what if the item selected was a relatively difficult one? Students who may have been able to answer less difficult items do not have an opportunity to demonstrate their actual ability levels. Finally, having more items on objective tests lessens the influence of guessing on the total score. Not helpful, however, is adding items that are either very difficult or very easy.

Keep in mind that the number of similar independent items or tasks, not simply the length of the assessment, is important in enhancing reliability. Thus, several shorter assessments usually provide a more reliable result than one or two long assessments. This is not to say that long assessments are not appropriate. It's just that it would be hard to justify end-of-course or unit grades on the basis of even a few different assessments. Teachers, by and large, are more interested in the reliability of the decision, grade, or final outcome than in a single assessment, so, from a practical standpoint, the principle of more assessment tasks for good reliability is important.

Difficulty of Assessment Items

Here is one of my favorite examples of test item difficulty. Is there a difference in the difficulty level of the following items that assess the same knowledge?

Which of the following is the state capital of Michigan?

a. Miami
b. New York
c. Lansing
d. Atlanta

Which of the following is the state capital of Michigan?

a. Grand Rapids
b. Detroit
c. Ann Arbor
d. Lansing

Obviously, the ability of a student to get the correct answer is a function of the difficulty of the items. If all the items are very easy or very hard, traditional reliability indexes will be low. High reliability correlations are obtained when there is a mix of difficulty in the items, with most ranging from 40% to 70% of the students obtaining correct answers. At least, this is typical for large-scale assessments. In the classroom, teachers typically build tests that are much easier. It does make sense to err on the side of leniency because teachers want to provide students a fair opportunity to show what they know and can do. Also, very difficult tests encourage guessing, which lowers reliability.

Quality of Assessment Items and Tasks

Naturally, the quality of the items and tasks is important for reliability. If the items are poorly worded, are misleading, have poor distracters, or do not discriminate well between known masters and nonmasters, then reliability will suffer. Because teachers do not usually pretest items, they determine that there is a problem only after the assessment has been completed. At this point, it is fine to eliminate that item and rescore the assessment for all the students (even if that means working with a total score other than 10, 20, 25, 50, or 100!). Once the scoring is complete, teachers can do an item analysis to determine which items will need to be revised for the future. Performance assessment tasks also need to be evaluated after students' responses have been recorded to get an indication of the quality of the task.

Objectivity in Scoring

Objectivity in assessment can refer either to the nature of the item (e.g., selected-response, such as multiple-choice) or to the nature of the scoring. Here, the interest is in the degree of objectivity in the scoring procedures. With objective items, this is clear because the scoring is highly objective and has little error. Constructed-response items, such as essays, papers, projects, and performance assessments, are subject to different degrees of scoring error, depending on the nature of the question and the scoring procedures. Fill-in-the-blank constructed-response items are scored fairly objectively, with little scorer error expected. Student responses and products that are subject to greater scorer bias, however, can have a detrimental effect on reliability. In many large-scale state testing programs, performance assessments have tended to show weak reliability for this reason. The key is in careful training of the scorers and careful development of scoring criteria that easily discriminate among different levels of performance.

Differences Among Individuals Assessed

Just as traditional reliability indices depend on a good spread of scores, they also depend on having a group that has a spread of knowledge, ability, or skill being assessed. That is, if everyone who is assessed has the same knowledge, ability, or skill level, a reliability correlation coefficient based on that group will be low. This principle poses a difficulty for teachers who are striving to get all students to a mastery level, because once that occurs, the reliability coefficient of the scores may seem low. In this case, reliability of the decision is helpful. Even then, however, if all students show mastery, there is insufficient information to determine what was *not* known or demonstrated. This principle helps explain why large-scale tests typically report "stronger" reliability than classroom tests. Large-scale test development includes a more heterogeneous sample of students than is typically found in the classroom.

Standard Error of Measurement

I would be remiss if I did not address *standard error of measurement* (SEM) in this chapter. As you recall, reliability is all about error. The SEM provides one approach to specifying the magnitude of the error in units used in the assessment when interpreting individual scores. Although we as test users know that error is present in every educational assessment, we are able to estimate error only on the basis of observed results of an assessment. We never know for sure what type or amount of error has actually influenced each observed score. Therefore, we *estimate* the degree of error that is probable, given the reliability of the test and the spread of scores, and call it SEM.

A useful way to think about SEM is to imagine what would happen if a student took the same test over and over again. Because of error, the scores received would not be the same. Suppose the obtained scores were 75, 78, 72, 74, and 75. Which one of these would be closest to the real knowledge or skill of the student? We can't know for sure. But we *do* know that the student's real knowledge or skill is probably between 72 and 78. It could even be reported as 75 + or -3. The actual calculation of SEM is more precise than this example, but this illustration provides a way to think about the principle conceptually.

In the discussion of interpretation of standardized tests in Chapter 6, I will come back to SEM because it is a key concept in making accurate inferences from these types of tests. Classroom tests rarely include the SEM, but software programs are available to do it rather easily.

Practical Suggestions for Classroom Assessment

So what does all this have to say to teachers who need some practical guidelines to improve the reliability of their assessments? One reality is that teachers give many assessments, which, although individually may not have established reliability evidence, when totaled at the end of the unit or semester can result in a reliable overall judgment. Given that most teachers will not be calculating correlations, the following suggestions will be of benefit:

- Motivate students to put forth their best effort on assessments.

- Use a sufficient number of items or tasks. A minimum of five items is needed to assess a single trait or skill.

- Construct items, scoring criteria, and tasks that clearly differentiate students on what is being assessed, and make the criteria public.

- Make sure procedures for scoring constructed-response items are consistently applied to all students.

- Use independent raters or observers to score a sample of student responses, and check consistency with your evaluations.

- Build in as much objectivity in the scoring as possible and still maintain the integrity of what is being assessed.

- Continue assessments until the results are consistent.

- Eliminate or reduce external sources of error.

- Use shorter assessments more frequently than fewer long assessments.

- Use several types of assessment tasks or methods of assessment.

- Use the same assessments over again.

- Use clearly identified anchors and other examples to illustrate scoring criteria.

- To the extent possible, standardize assessment and scoring protocols and procedures.

- Keep an item and task bank or file; don't release tests to students for them to keep.

The most important aspect of reliability to keep in mind when designing and interpreting educational assessments is that error, to some degree, is part of every score. The goal is to understand the nature and extent of this error and then include this information when using the scores for instructional decision making, grades, and curriculum evaluation.

CHAPTER 4

Fairness

The goal of assessment is to obtain a sound inference about what a student knows, understands, and can do. Such inferences can then lead to good decisions that enhance student learning and can also inform teachers, the public, and policymakers. Although the principles of reliability and validity have served well as the foundation of sound assessment, it has recently become evident that issues of fairness are equally important.

There are many ways to think about fairness in relation to educational assessment, and it is not possible to discuss all these complex issues in this book. A full consideration would explore testing in relation to broader social goals and legal and ethical issues. I will be concerned with fairness as reflected in the nature of assessments and the use of information generated from assessments in classrooms and schools.

What Is Fairness?

The term *fairness* can be defined from several perspectives (Heubert & Hauser, 1999). It can be defined broadly as a condition or situation in which assessments are not unduly influenced by factors unrelated to the learning objectives or standards that are being measured. Fairness can also be described as equitable treatment of those being assessed. Equity implies justness or fairness, which differs from equality (being the same). The term *bias* is often thought of as the opposite of fairness. Obviously, assessments should be free from bias, whether that bias is based on gender, race, socioeconomic status (SES), or other characteristics that may influence the performance being assessed. If some students have an advantage because of factors unrelated to what is being assessed, then the assessment is not fair.

Fair assessments are unbiased and nondiscriminatory, uninfluenced by irrelevant factors such as gender or race and by subjective factors such as the bias of a scorer. In other words, in a fair assessment, students have the opportunity to demonstrate their learning in a way such that their performance is not distorted by their race, gender, ethnic background, handicapping condition, or other factors unrelated to the purpose of the assessment. A fair assessment is also characterized by scoring that is not affected by these factors.

Unfair assessments result in performances that both underestimate and overestimate the traits being measured. A common example of unfair assessment is when particular groups of examinees are put at a disadvantage. This frequently occurs when there is something about the content of the assessment that makes it more difficult for students with certain characteristics. For example, suppose a test is designed to assess students' writing skills by asking them to respond to the following prompt:

> Write a short story about a boy who practices very hard to be good in basketball and makes the team.

This type of prompt may be easier for boys to respond to than for girls. The girls may score lower than boys not because they don't have the writing skills but because they are less familiar with this sport. This suggests that the test is biased against girls. On the other hand, boys may score higher because they have experience to draw from in writing their short stories. In either case, there is some distortion in the performance caused by a factor unrelated to what is being assessed. Another good example is a reading comprehension assessment in which the content of the reading passage favors one group over another. If the content is about a sailing experience, then examinees who live in a community in which sailing is ubiquitous would have an easier time reading and understanding the passage than would examinees who know little about sailing.

Although it is impossible to completely remove all unfair aspects of an assessment for every student, teachers and administrators can do much to ensure that assessments are as fair as possible. We can also understand the various ways fairness can affect our interpretations and uses of assessment results. This is particularly important given the increasingly diverse characteristics of students and increased emphasis on identification of students with special needs. Because of these conditions, fairness is just as important as the standbys of validity and reliability.

Fairness as It Relates to Student Knowledge of Learning Targets and Assessments

Have you ever taken a test and then thought, "If I had known the test was going to cover this content, I would have studied it"? I know I have. A fair assessment is one in which it is clear to students what will and will not be tested, what test format will be used, and how the test will be scored. The goal is not to trick, fool, or outguess students about what is assessed. Rather, teachers need to be clear and relatively specific about the nature of the target students need to learn and how that performance will be scored. When this is communicated to all students *prior to instruction* and in a *public way,* students, as well as parents, know what needs to be learned. This approach helps students know what to study and focus on as well as how to study. For example, if students know that they will need to show their work on a mathematics test, they will practice showing their work and, it is hoped, receive feedback about what they show. If students know that they will have an essay test that will be graded with a known set of scoring criteria, they will pull together their thoughts in a way that organizes the content to respond to the criteria, rather than simply memorizing content.

Let's look at another example in more depth to illustrate the importance of specificity and clarity in learning targets, the test itself, and scoring criteria. Suppose you are going to teach a unit on cultural diversity. Here is the first learning target you identify:

Students will be able to identify and learn about different cultures.

You tell students that they will be tested on this learning target at the end of the unit. This information, although shared with students, is so general and vague that it indicates little about what will be learned, the test format, and the scoring criteria. Students are left guessing about what they really need to learn, what will be on the test, how they will be tested, and how the test will be scored. Consider the next more specific target and description of assessment:

Students will identify characteristics of several cultures and be able to show how they are both similar and different.

You inform students that the assessment will be described as a constructed-response test in which students will list the characteristics of each of the cultures and indicate ways they are similar and ways they are different. With this information, students have a much better idea about what to learn and how their learning will be assessed. There is much less guessing based on idiosyncratic student differences, which makes the assessment more fair.

Here, the target is even more specific:

Students will identify six characteristics of three cultures, explain how each culture differs from the others, and explain the implications of these differences and similarities on freedom of expression and tolerance.

Students are told that the assessment will require them to list the six characteristics of each culture, explain how the cultures are the same and how they are different, and explain how differences and similarities in the cultures may affect freedom of expression and tolerance in everyday life. Now students have a clear idea what they will learn and how they will be required to demonstrate their learning. This type of target is more fair because it takes the ambiguity out of the process, replacing it with clarity and specificity.

Another good illustration of the importance of the targets is learning to drive. Students take a driver education course with the expectation that certain specific skills will be tested. It would be unfair if students were taught to drive using an automatic transmission and then, when asked to demonstrate their skills, had to do so with a manual transmission. What would be fair is telling students at the beginning of the course that they had to learn to drive competently with both a manual and an automatic transmission.

One of the positive consequences of ensuring that students know the learning targets, the test format, and scoring criteria in advance is that it can help motivate students and help them obtain a learning goal orientation. Recent research has indicated that students are intrinsically motivated when they learn for mastery, rather than for mere performance (Ames, 1992; Dweck & Leggett, 1988). With a *learning* or *mastery* goal orientation, students are motivated by a focus on mastering a task according to established standards, developing new skills, improving competence, and gaining understanding and insight. In addition, when students assume a mastery orientation, they are more likely to see a significant link between their effort, feedback, and the outcome. This link promotes more internal attributions for success (e.g., reasons for success such as ability and effort). Finally, mastery-oriented goals lead to greater effort and involvement as well as interest and positive attitudes (Pintrich & Schunk, 1996).

In contrast, when students have vague information about the learning targets, the type of assessment, and scoring criteria, they tend to assume a performance goal orientation. Students are likely to focus on the consequences of the outcome, that is, a grade or some other recognition or reward, with relatively little concern about the level of understanding or learning. When only general information about the targets and assessments is provided, students find it more difficult to see the link between their effort, feedback, and the outcome.

The principle of goal orientation is nicely illustrated with gymnastics. The targets are clear and specific, and the criteria by which gymnasts are judged are public and well understood by the athletes and coaches. This results in a learning orientation that encourages intrinsic motivation. When gymnasts are judged, the assessment is fair because the athletes know that the same rules apply to all and they know, in advance, how their performances will be judged. Gymnasts prepare a specific routine to demonstrate their skills, knowing ahead of time that the routine is appropriate. Can you imagine gymnasts attending a meet not knowing the nature of the specific routine they should perform or how it will be judged?

Fairness as It Relates to Opportunity to Learn

Opportunity to learn is providing students adequate time and appropriate instruction to enable them to obtain mastery. It is not fair if students are held accountable for knowledge and skills that have not been taught or that have not been part of the curriculum. This is especially troublesome when interpretations about the quality of schools or teaching are made on the basis of student achievement tests. When students have not had an adequate opportunity to learn the knowledge and skills covered by the test, they are likely to get low scores. Serious decisions based on these low scores, such as school accreditation, teacher employment, and withholding of high school diplomas, are not valid because of lack of opportunity to learn. It is not so much a matter of accuracy because students indeed may not have the knowledge and skills, but the consequences are inappropriate.

At the classroom level, opportunity to learn is directly related to what teachers do and the instructional resources provided. Did students know how to learn the targeted knowledge and skills? Were there adequate resources for all students, or were some students excluded from use of needed resources? Was there adequate supervision at home for homework, or did some students fail to receive needed practice? Did the lessons implemented cover what was on the test? Has illness or absenteeism made it difficult for some students to learn the material? How can a student be held accountable for content and skills that could not be taught because the student was ill? How adequate was the instruction? Is it fair to hold students accountable for poor instruction? These types of questions raise issues related to opportunity to learn. Obviously, opportunity to learn is a matter of judgment and of degree, but there should at least be guidelines to identify situations that clearly limit students' opportunities so that this information can become part of the interpretation of the scores. For example, it would not make much sense to make a negative judgment about a teacher or school on the basis of student test scores based on knowledge and skills that the teacher or school simply did not include as part of instruction.

Opportunity to learn takes on even greater importance when assessment results are used for making decisions based on the relative performance of different examinees. This is done regularly in selecting students for special programs and for allocating scarce resources. In these situations, it is critical that all students have equal access to what is being assessed and equal opportunity to prepare for the assessment. The assessment conditions and access to test preparation materials should also be the same for all students. These conditions are best achieved when the nature of the assessment is well-known long before it is administered and when administration of the assessment is standardized (e.g., same directions and procedures for all students). If some students have prior access to secured tests, it would not be fair to compare their scores with the scores of other students who did not have such access.

Fairness as It Relates to Student Prerequisite Knowledge and Skills

It is not fair to assess students on content or skills that require prerequisite knowledge, understanding, or skills that they do not possess. Such knowledge and skills are often referred to as *enabling behaviors* because they are necessary but not sufficient for demonstrating the targeted learning. For instance, writing skills are considered enablers for being able to respond to an essay question, just as reading comprehension is needed to answer a social studies test. Teachers don't want the assessment to measure differences on the enabling knowledge and skills that students bring to the assessment. How can teachers avoid this potential source of unfairness?

First, it is important to identify the knowledge and skills that are needed as prerequisites. For example, suppose a mathematics unit focused on reasoning skills related to fractions, and the items on the test required students to read short paragraphs to solve the problems. Successful performance on such a test depends on students' skill in adding, subtracting, multiplying, and dividing fractions *and* on students' reading skills. Students would be unable to demonstrate their reasoning if they could not read and understand the paragraphs, even if they were proficient at working with fractions.

Second, teachers need to have a good understanding of the prerequisite knowledge and skills that their students can demonstrate. Sometimes, this is done with formal pretests or other structured assessment, but more often, teachers use informal assignments and oral questioning to get a sense of whether students have the needed knowledge and skills.

A different but equally important type of prerequisite skill is concerned with test taking. *Test-taking* skills are those that allow students to maximize their performance by not being distracted by format or approach. For example, if a new question format is used, students need to become familiar with that format prior to the assessment. If students are going to be using Scantron forms for the first time, they need practice in using these forms. More general test-taking skills include the following:

- Paying careful attention to general directions and how answers are to be made
- Paying attention when reading or listening to items
- Pacing so that not too much time is spent on one item
- Being willing to skip difficult items initially and return to them later
- Answering all items if all are included in the scoring
- Learning how to guess the correct answer
- Learning how to omit wrong answers on multiple-choice tests rather than looking for the right answer

- Checking so that item and answer numbers match
- Checking answers if time permits
- Organizing essay answers before writing them
- Realizing that some items will be very difficult and not being too concerned when this occurs
- Knowing the scoring criteria for performance assessments
- Knowing acceptable formats for completing performance assessments
- Knowing how to prepare for the test
- Knowing how to handle test anxiety

Another set of skills has been identified as *test-wise* skills. These skills help the examinee identify correct answers by errors in test questions or by clues to the correct answer. Such deficiencies are common in poorly constructed multiple-choice test items. Should students be taught the following skills to maximize scores?

- Look for grammatical clues such as inappropriate use of *a* and *an*.

  In a study of the effect of training on performance, the training is an
  a. dependent variable
  b. independent variable
  c. continuous variable
  d. control variable

- Look for vague words such as *often* or *usually* that may indicate the correct answer. Absolutes are typically incorrect.

  In an experiment, the independent variable is
  a. measured at the end
  b. always matched with a control variable
  c. almost always categorical
  d. the most important variable for understanding the result

- Look for options that are longest or most precise.

  If a quasi-experimental study examines the effect of training on performance, what possible extraneous variable would need to be controlled if at all possible?
  a. Differences between the groups that could account for differences obtained on the dependent variable
  b. The situations in which the performance is tested
  c. The directions given to the subjects
  d. The time of day of the training

Should students be trained in these types of skills? Although all students clearly need test-taking skills, there may be some hesitancy in teaching test-wise skills. What is important for fairness is that all students have the same degree of test-wiseness. To ensure this, it seems to me that it is desirable to inform all students about these types of skills. More generally, students should be familiar with the format and type of question and response that will be needed on an assessment. This is often accomplished by giving students practice questions or showing them examples done by students in previous years. This doesn't mean teaching the test, that is, using examples during test preparation that are identical to what will be on the test. But it does make sense to teach *to* the test in the sense of teaching students the content and skills that will be assessed.

Fairness as It Relates to Absence of Bias in Assessment Tasks and Scoring

A fair assessment is one in which neither the assessment tasks nor the scoring contains bias. This type of influence is perhaps the best known source of unfairness in testing. *Bias* can be defined as qualities of the assessment that distort performance because of the student's ethnicity, gender, race, religious background, SES, or other characteristics. Such distortion, as pointed out earlier, can distort by either raising or lowering test scores, but usually bias is associated with a negative impact (hence the phrase "biased against"). Popham (1995) has identified two forms of assessment bias: offensiveness and unfair penalization.

Offensiveness

Offensiveness occurs when the content of the assessment offends, upsets, angers, distresses, or otherwise creates negative emotions for students of particular subgroups. The negative effect influences the performance of these students, lowering their scores and reducing validity. The distressed students are distracted from what is being assessed and focus more on the offensive content. Offensiveness is particularly unfair when stereotypes of particular subgroups are present. Suppose a test question portrays women in low-status, low-paying jobs and men in professional positions. Women taking the test may be offended by the negative portrayal. The distress leads to less than optimal performance, resulting in scores that underestimate the actual knowledge of the students. Some men taking the test will also be offended by such content. Table 4.1 shows some additional examples of test items that may create offensiveness.

Table 4.1 Examples of Offensiveness in the Content of Assessments

Ethnicity	Juan picks beans for a living. He receives 20 cents for every bushel he picks. Juan picked 20 bushels a day for 2 weeks. How much should he be paid for his work?
Gender	The president of General Mix has held his present position for 10 years. His secretary has been with him for all 10 years. She has received a 4% raise each year, whereas the president has received a 10% raise each year. If the president started at a salary of $100,000 and his secretary at $10,000, what is the current difference in their salaries?
Race	Write a 2-page essay on the following: African American teenagers constitute 10% of the population, but 30% of the crime in this city is committed by African American teenagers. How do you explain the difference in these percentages?
Religion	Write a 200-word essay on how right-wing Republican Christians have influenced the outcome of the past two presidential elections with their extremist views.

In large-scale testing, item-writing and review procedures are used to eliminate any offensiveness in the content of the assessments. In classroom testing, however, it is more likely that such offensiveness will occur. Teachers simply do not have the time or resources to conduct systematic reviews of test content. For assessments that have important consequences, it is advisable for teachers to ask a colleague to review the content to look specifically for offensiveness, as well as other types of bias. Because teachers are often unaware that the content may be biased by unconsciously including wording or characterizations that may offend some students, a review by a colleague is helpful.

Unfair Penalization

Unfair penalization refers to bias due to the content of the assessment. The result is that the content makes the assessment more difficult for some students than for others. In other words, bias is present when a disadvantage is given to one group or individual because of gender, SES, race, language, or other characteristic. This is the type of unfairness when the simple phrase "this is a biased test" is used. The content makes it harder for some students to score well because of factors unrelated to what they are learning in school.

Suppose you take a test that measures your aptitude by using mostly rural, farm-oriented content. The items cover such topics as types of cows and pigs,

Table 4.2 Examples of Unfair Penalization

Socioeconomic background	Students are required to pass a computer competency test to be promoted to high school.
Socioeconomic background	Students are required to work in small groups to plan a trip from their school to Washington, D.C. In their plans, they must include expenses and an itinerary of activities. The plans will be graded on comprehensiveness and practicality.
Religion	What is the Koran?
Location	Write a persuasive essay about using hiking as recreation. In your answer, compare hiking with sailing.
Gender	Dale Ernhart's car traveled at 180.5 miles per hour for the entire race. How many seconds did it take him to finish the 200-mile race?

farm equipment, and winter crops. If you grew up in a city or suburb, do you think your score would be as high as the scores of students who grew up on a farm? Similarly, is it fair to compare students whose primary language is Spanish with students whose primary language is English on English oral reading skills? Do test items containing sports content give boys an unfair advantage over girls because the boys are more familiar with sports? In each case, membership in a particular group or background unrelated to instruction influences the score. Further examples of unfair penalization are illustrated in Table 4.2.

For many years, large-scale standardized tests contained content (such as vocabulary, pictures, names, and situations) that was more familiar to Caucasian students from middle- to upper-SES communities than to minority students from low-SES communities, simply because of Caucasian middle- and upper-SES students' everyday life experiences. This meant that lower-SES minorities would be unfairly penalized and score lower on the tests. Publishing companies are now careful to exclude any content that may unfairly penalize students of certain groups, but it is virtually impossible to remove all types of bias from such tests. Questions need to be written with some type of content, and invariably this content will unfairly penalize some students to some degree. The possible bias that may result from a specific test given to certain students should be taken into account to promote accurate interpretation.

Just because test scores are different for specific subgroups, the assessment is not necessarily biased. For example, if Hispanic students score lower, overall, on the SAT, this does not mean that these tests are culturally biased and unfairly penalize Hispanic students. The actual content of the tests needs to be analyzed to determine bias.

In the increasingly diverse culture of the United States, student differences reflected in vocabulary, prior experience, skills, and values may influence both formal and informal assessments. Consider the impact of the following cultural differences (McMillan, in press):

- Knowledge from the immediate environment of the student provides a vocabulary as well as an indication of the importance or relevance of assessment tasks (e.g., large city, ethnic neighborhood, rural, coastal, and farm).

- Depending on the culture in which the student lives, there may be different norms and rules for sharing beliefs, discussion, asking questions, taking turns, and expressing opinions.

- Respect and politeness may be expressed differently by students from different cultures (e.g., silence, squinting as a way to say no, looking up or down when asked a question, and not looking into another's eyes when answering a question).

- Learning style differences may influence a student's confidence and motivation to complete certain assessment tasks (e.g., preferences for working alone or in a group, learning by listening or reading, ability to think analytically or globally, and tendency to answer reflectively or impulsively).

The influences of these differences will be minimized to the extent that teachers and administrators first understand them, then review assessments for possible bias, and finally incorporate possible limitations because of bias in their interpretations of student performance. The differential impact of cultures is also minimized by using multiple assessments with varying formats. This helps students show their progress toward achieving the learning target and results in more valid inferences about students. If one assessment technique or approach advantages students from one type of background, another technique may be a disadvantage to those same students. Using different types of assessments provides a balance to the others. For example, students who perform poorly on an oral test may perform well on a written test. This points out an important principle in all assessments: *Never rely solely on one method of assessment.* This doesn't mean that you should arbitrarily select different assessment methods. Use a variety of assessments that provide the fairest indication of student performance for all students.

Fairness as It Relates to Avoiding Stereotypes

In making judgments about students, it is only natural to form and use beliefs related to how students are likely to perform. These beliefs about what students are capable of knowing or doing are called *expectations*. Expectations are not necessarily bad. Realistic, accurate expectations are helpful in designing appropriate instruction. Expectations that are biased because of membership in a particular group, however, need to be avoided. When such expectations occur, the stereotypes will influence expectations and the nature of subjective judgments. Here are some examples of stereotypes in education:

"Jocks aren't very bright."

"Girls do better in most subjects than boys."

"Girls do poorly in mathematics."

"Kids from the south side are great athletes but are weak academically."

"A single-parent home means the father won't be involved."

In its most negative form, inappropriate use of stereotypes is self-fulfilling and detrimental. For example, if a teacher has a stereotype about students from a certain ethnic background and that stereotype is translated into behaviors toward the students, then the students may interpret that behavior as an indicator of their capability. Should students perform consistently with the communicated level of performance, the teacher or administrator will in turn interpret this as evidence to reinforce the original stereotype. A useful way to think about such stereotypes is by when they are made in relation to assessments, that is, prior to, during, or after instruction.

Stereotypes Prior to Instruction or Assessment

A hallmark of an effective teacher is to match instructional activities with the capabilities that students bring to school. The teacher needs to assess these capabilities prior to making final decisions about instruction. Such assessment occurs before school begins, continues during the first week or two of the new school year, and occurs again during the year when beginning new units. During these "preinstructional" times, information is gathered and interpreted to answer such questions as the following:

Do students have the content knowledge and skills to handle the new material?

In what aspects of the content will students be most interested?

How can I take into account backgrounds of students to maximize motivation?

How much heterogeneity will there be in the class? How can I accommodate students who are behind others?

Stereotypes develop when interpretations and conclusions are based on fragmented or partial information. Consider the following examples:

> "John comes from a single-parent family; he will have difficulty completing his homework."

> "Tanya is from the low-income area of the city; she will be behind in mathematics."

> "This class has mostly boys; it's going to be difficult to control."

> "These students from Mott Middle School will need remediation."

> "Carol has dirty clothes; she probably didn't get a good breakfast and will probably have difficulty concentrating in class."

In each case, judgments are made on the basis of stereotypes, rather than on evidence specific to each individual or group. This is unfair to the students.

To design the most effective instructional experiences, it is helpful to gather as much evidence as possible about student backgrounds and capabilities. When this is done systematically by reviewing school records, test scores, and recommendations from previous teachers, it is more likely that undesirable stereotypes will be avoided. Stereotypes are also avoided if teachers wait until they have had some interaction with each student before making summary judgments. This interaction occurs during the first week or so and, when added to other information, can provide a complete and accurate assessment. When there is consistency among several sources of information, the resultant expectation will be more accurate.

Stereotypes During Formative Assessment

Formative assessments are made during instruction. As instructional activities are being implemented, there is a need to constantly gather "evidence" from students that is focused on how much students are paying attention and learning. This continuous monitoring provides feedback to the teacher to assess progress toward understanding the content or accomplishing the skill. Teachers typically use informal observation of students to accomplish formative assessments. This involves looking at and listening to students and then interpreting their behavior. Both verbal and nonverbal student behavior is important. The goal is to obtain an accurate picture of where students are in relation to the lesson and learning targets, and stereotypes will interfere with an accurate interpretation of these observations.

Stereotypes can influence formative assessment in a general, continuous way or can be more specific to particular situations. If teachers have a stereotype about boys being on task less than girls, in general, teachers may tend to monitor boys more closely than girls. If there is an expectation that students who live in poverty will, in general, have more difficulty learning the content, then that stereotype may affect the way the teacher interprets questions asked by these students. Asian American students are often stereotyped as high achievers. If this means that silence from these students is interpreted to mean that they understand, while silence from other students means they are bored, then the stereotype has interfered with an accurate formative assessment.

On a more specific level, teachers can form stereotypes about certain students. General opinions of individual students as "able" or "bright" or "smart," on the one hand, may contrast with opinions of other students labeled as "unable," "not very bright," or even "dumb." This stereotyping can form a "halo" for each student that may distort subsequent evaluations to be consistent with the nature of the halo. For example, a student viewed as bright may give an answer that will be interpreted on the basis of the halo as much as on the basis of the quality of the answer. It is also possible for teachers' formative assessments to be influenced by primacy effects, in which initial impressions have a distorting effect on later assessments, and by recency effects, in which interpretations are unduly influenced by the most recent observation.

Stereotypes During Summative Assessment

Stereotypes distort summative assessments most in the scoring of student responses. When constructed-response assessments are scored, teachers use their judgments of the responses to interpret student progress and learning. These judgments require subjectivity to a certain extent, and it is in this subjectivity that stereotypes can lead to unfair evaluations. Suppose a teacher is grading responses to an essay question. Will knowing the name of the student completing the response mean that some type of stereotype of this student will influence the evaluation (e.g., "She never does well on these types of assignments" or "She always does great on essays")? That is definitely possible. Is it likely that a teacher would evaluate a performance assessment more positively for some students than for others solely on the basis of characteristics unrelated to the assessment? For example, will student athletes receive lower evaluations because a teacher has a stereotype that athletes are more concerned about their sport than about school achievement? Are students who belong to the drama club stereotyped as better actors and actresses, so that when judgments are made about who will be assigned different parts in a play, this stereotype influences the judges to select the drama club students for the best roles?

These types of stereotypes can be avoided, resulting in a more fair assessment, if scoring criteria are as specific and explicit as possible. The more general and vague the scoring criteria, the more opportunity there is for stereotypes to influence the judgments that are made. When grading students' constructed-responses, it is best to grade one question at a time for all students, and, if possible, grade them without knowing the names of the students. Examples or outlines of answers should be generated to act as anchors in the judgment process.

It is also helpful to review the performance of test takers of different races, gender, and ethnic background to determine if performance is related to these characteristics. If, for example, all the female examinees do well and all the male examinees do poorly, there may be something in the scoring related to gender stereotypes that is unfair. As indicated earlier, differential performance by different groups doesn't mean there is bias, but if there is bias, it will be reflected in this way. The summative assessments, then, provide data that may indicate bias or stereotypes.

Fairness as It Relates to Accommodating Special Needs

One of the most challenging aspects of teaching is accommodating students with mild disabilities who are now routinely mainstreamed into regular classes. From the standpoint of assessment of these students, it is important for legal, ethical, and instructional reasons to adapt assessment practices so that they are fair and unbiased. Legally, teachers are responsible for gathering information, through assessment, to identify students who may become eligible for special education services. Assessments are used by teachers to provide information needed to determine if students are making satisfactory progress toward meeting learning targets specified in their IEPs. For both of these responsibilities, the law requires that the selection and administration of assessments must not be racially or culturally discriminatory. At a minimum, the law requires the following:

1. Personnel administering tests must be trained.

2. Assessments must be in the child's native language.

3. Assessments must identify specific needs, not a single, general indication of ability or aptitude.

4. Assessment materials and administration must accurately indicate aptitude or achievement without discriminating against the child's disability.

5. No single score or procedure is sufficient as a sole criterion for determining an IEP.

6. A multidisciplinary team needs to assess the child in all areas related to the suspected disability.

These provisions mean that assessment must be planned and implemented so that the score is determined by the trait being assessed and not by the disability. That is, it would be unfair to use a test written in English to determine that a student, whose primary language is Chinese, has low ability or aptitude. It would also be unfair to conclude that a student with a fine motor disability did not demonstrate understanding as reflected in an essay question because there was insufficient time for the student to write the answer. In other words, it is illegal for the score of the trait being assessed to be influenced by the disability.

Impacts of Disabilities on Assessment

Beyond these legal requirements, teachers need to make appropriate accommodations in classroom assessments because many disabilities affect test-taking abilities. Without such accommodations, scores are unlikely to be valid or reliable. Students with disabilities have specific difficulties that are directly related to assessment. These factors are summarized in Table 4.3.

Many students with even mild disabilities have difficulty with comprehension. This means that they may not understand directions well or remember a sequence of steps required to complete a task. This is especially troublesome for abstract tasks that require reasoning or other thinking skills. For example, a question such as "How is the Canadian government different from a socialistic form of government?" would be much more difficult than "What are the characteristics of a socialist form of government?" Auditory and visual difficulties can exacerbate limits to comprehension. If students have trouble processing verbal information quickly and accurately, or if visual and perceptual disabilities make it hard to discriminate letters and symbols, then comprehension is affected. During tests, many students with disabilities will be easily distracted by visual cues such as gestures or motions of others, which disrupt their visual focus and concentration.

Time can be a major difficulty for many students with disabilities. It simply takes these students longer to complete tests because of limitations related to how quickly they can understand and process information and record their answers. Timed or speeded tests, for example, may lead to increased levels of anxiety, especially if students are concerned that their disability will make it difficult to complete the task within given time limits.

Students with disabilities may be more sensitive to feelings of embarrassment than are other students. To avoid embarrassment, they often want to hide or disguise their disability so that they will not be singled out by peers. As a result, they may want to be treated like all other students. They may not ask questions about directions they do not understand or may hand in a test when others do even if they have not finished. Finally, the behavior of students with

Table 4.3 Factors That Affect the Assessment of Students With
Disabilities

Factor	*Impact on Assessment*
Poor comprehension	Understanding directions; completing assessments
Poor auditory skills	Understanding oral directions, assessment tasks, and questions; being distracted by noises
Poor visual skills	Understanding written directions, assessment tasks, and questions; decoding symbols and letters; being distracted by visual cues
Time constraints	Finishing assessments
Anxiety	Finishing assessments and being able to think clearly; demonstrating best work
Embarrassment	Finishing assessments; being reluctant to ask questions
Variability of behavior	Finishing assessments; demonstrating best work

disabilities may vary significantly from one setting to another or from one time to another. Consequently, teachers need to be flexible with assessments and realize that at any one time, a disability may pose extreme difficulties for the student.

Assessment Accommodations

Assessment accommodations for students with disabilities can be grouped into three categories: test directions, test construction, and test administration. Directions can be modified in the following ways:

- Read written directions slowly, and give students ample opportunity to ask questions.
- Keep directions simple and short.
- Give examples of how to answer questions if students are not familiar with the format.
- Give separate directions for each section of the test.
- Give one direction in each sentence.

- Check students' understanding of the directions.
- Monitor the students during the assessment.

Tests should be constructed to include plenty of white space, a font size that is not too small, and double spacing. Different sections should be clearly differentiated, with only one type of question on each page. Each page of the test should be numbered. Other accommodations to the format of the test depend on the type of item, as illustrated in the following examples.

Short-Answer, Essay, and Completion Items

Short-answer and essay items may be difficult for students with disabilities because of the organization, reasoning, and writing skills required. Long, complicated questions should be avoided. If words such as *compare, contrast,* and *discuss* are used, they need to be clearly defined. Limit the number of questions, and allow students to outline their answers. Some students may need to give an audio-recorded, rather than a written, answer, and all students with disabilities will need sufficient time to complete their answers. Word banks can be provided on a separate sheet to aid memory. Provide plenty of space for students to record their answers.

Multiple-Choice and Binary-Choice Items

Have students circle their answers, rather than writing the letter next to the item or transferring their answers to a separate sheet. Make sure that response categories are arranged vertically, not horizontally. Usually, the number of alternatives in a multiple-choice item should be limited to four, and wording such as "a and b but not d" and "either a or c" should be avoided. Any negatively stated stems or alternatives should be used sparingly. If words such as "not" are used, they should be highlighted with bold print and/or underlines.

Performance Assessments

The first accommodation with performance assessments that will need to be made is with the directions. What is expected needs to be clearly explained with examples and a reasonable time frame. Certain skills may need to be modified if the disability interferes directly with performance of the skill. Assistance needs to be provided in cases in which the disability makes it difficult for the student to perform the skill. For example, a speech impediment may affect a student's ability to give a speech or oral report. In this situation, the student may need assistance in organizing and delivering the speech or report.

Portfolios may be an ideal type of assessment for students with disabilities because the assignments and requirements can be individualized to show progress in whatever time frame is appropriate. Portfolios could be adapted by modifying requirements to include those that would be least affected by the disability. Reflections by both the student and teacher could be included that specifically address progress despite the presence of the disability.

Adaptations in Administration of Assessments

Many of the adaptations that need to be made in the administration of an assessment are dependent on the nature of the disability. In general, the goal is to use procedures that lessen or remove the negative impact of the disability on the trait being assessed. Some of the suggestions for adaptations are based on common sense (e.g., for students who have difficulty hearing, be sure that the directions are written; for students with a visual difficulty, make sure directions are given orally). It is best to place a Testing: Do Not Disturb sign on the classroom door to discourage visitors and other distractions. Some students may need to be removed from the regular classroom and taken to a separate room in which distractions are minimal. If someone can monitor the assessment, the student will have more opportunities to ask questions and be less likely to be embarrassed when asking for clarification or other assistance.

Classroom teachers who are unsure about appropriate assessment accommodations should check with the special education specialist in the school. This will help the teachers understand the nature of the disabilities and what specific accommodations are appropriate.

In Table 4.4, suggested adaptations are summarized according to different types of disabilities. For many students, however, several of these difficulties will need to be addressed (e.g., students with an auditory disability may also have comprehension, anxiety, and time constraint difficulties).

Overall Judgments About Fairness

Unbiased and nondiscriminatory assessments are developed and implemented by administrators who first know what to look for and then match this analysis of assessment tasks and scoring with student characteristics. The checklist in Figure 4.1 is provided to help you make a quick verification of the possible ways assessments may be unfair. As teachers and administrators, we

Table 4.4 Adaptations in Administering Assessments

Disability or Difficulty	Assessment Adaptations
Poor comprehension	• Give test directions both orally and in written form. • Double-check student understanding. • Avoid making long talks before the assessment is administered. • Allow students to audio-record answers. • Do not correct constructed-response answers for grammar or spelling. • Remind students to check that all questions have been answered. • Allow the use of multiplication tables and calculators for math problems. • Read the test to the student. • Provide an outline for essay question responses. • Use mostly objective items.
Auditory difficulties	• Use written rather than oral questions. • Read slowly when administering an oral test, enunciating and sounding out clearly. • Arrange for students to take the assessment in a quiet place. • Stress the importance of being quiet to all students.
Visual difficulties	• Give directions orally. • Give the assessment orally or by tape. • Allow students to take the test orally. • Seat the student away from visual distractions, such as windows and doors. • Do not have students milling around the room after completing the assessment. • Meet class visitors at the door and talk in the hallway.
Time constraint difficulties	• Allow plenty of time to complete the assessment. • Provide breaks in lengthy assessments. • Give different parts of the assessment on different days. • Do not use timed or speeded tests.
Anxiety	• Allow plenty of time to complete the assessment. • Avoid adding pressure by telling students to "hurry up and finish." • Do not threaten students with results of the assessment. • Do not use assessments as punishment for poor behavior.

Table 4.4 Continued

Disability or Difficulty	Assessment Adaptations
	• Give a practice assessment or practice items. • Allow students to take a retest. • Do not threaten dire consequences for poor performance. • Emphasize internal attributions of ability and effort for previous work. • Do not use a few major assessments; use many smaller assessments. • Do not use norm-referenced interpretations.
Embarrassment	• Make modified assessments look like the regular assessments. • Avoid calling attention to students with disabilities if they need special assistance. • Monitor all students in the class the same way. • Avoid giving special attention to students with disabilities when handing out a test or other assessment. • Confer privately with students about appropriate accommodations prior to giving the assessment. • Do not single out students with disabilities when returning assessments.
Variability of behavior	• Allow retesting. • Allow students to reschedule assessments for another day. • Monitor closely to determine if behavior is preventing students from doing their best work.

SOURCE: Adapted from *Adapting Instruction for Mainstreamed and At-Risk Students*, by J. Wood, Copyright © 1992. Adapted by permission of Prentice-Hall, Inc., Upper Saddle River, NJ.

want all students to have an equal chance of showing what they know and can do, and we want the content of the assessment and the scoring to be unbiased. Even one serious unfair quality of an assessment may render the results invalid. Ask yourself this question: Would all students with the same level of knowledge, understanding, and skill, regardless of their differences or handicapping traits, demonstrate similar performance? If the answer is "yes," then the assessment is probably fair. If the answer is "no" or "I'm not sure," then there is reason to believe that the assessment is unfair.

✓   Did students know the learning targets and nature of the assessment *prior to instruction?*

✓   Did students have reasonable opportunity to learn what was assessed?

✓   Did students have needed prerequisite knowledge and skills?

✓   Did students have appropriate test-taking skills?

✓   Was there any offensiveness in the assessment?

✓   Was there any unfair penalization in the assessment?

✓   Were stereotypes avoided?

✓   Were accommodations made for students with disabilities?

Figure 4.1. Checklist of Considerations for Determining Fairness of Assessments

CHAPTER 5

Understanding and Using Numerical Data

Even if you could avoid this chapter and its emphasis on data, numbers, and even "dreaded statistics," you wouldn't want to. This is because it is essential to have a good understanding of the meaning of data and how data can be used to improve instruction. Broadly speaking, *data* can be defined as summary information. This chapter examines numerical data, scores that are obtained when student performance is measured. Here are six reasons why an understanding of numerical data is essential:

1. Numerical data can be used to efficiently summarize and describe a large number of scores.

2. Numerical data are important in determining student grades.

3. Numerical data are used in reporting standardized test scores; an accurate interpretation and the valid use of these scores depend on understanding the data.

4. Numerical data are used extensively in describing validity, reliability, norms, item statistics, and other characteristics of tests and surveys; adequate analysis and interpretation of the quality of tests and surveys depend on understanding numerical data.

5. With an increasing emphasis on school accountability, numerical data are used extensively in school report cards and other reports; teachers and administrators need to be able to understand and evaluate these data.

6. Most research uses numerical data; an understanding of the nature of data helps interpret and use research findings on topics of interest.

I will begin the discussion by reviewing the nature of scores, the most fundamental and important way data are summarized.

Types of Scores

Several types of scores are commonly used in measurement. The *raw score* typically indicates the actual number of items a student has answered correctly. If 15 of 20 items are correct, then the raw score is 15. This is based on the simple frequency of items. A *frequency* is a count of items or of students. Frequency can refer to the number of students obtaining a specific score or range of scores. For example, if 10 students obtained a score of 75 and 10 students scored 78, the frequency of scores from 75 to 78 is 20.

Percentage indicates the number of items or students per hundred. Thus, if there are 25 items on a test and a student answered 20 of the items correctly, the student answered 80% of the items correctly. Similarly, if 15 students in a class of 30 students fail a test, 50% of the students in the class fail. Percentage is calculated with division and multiplication. Simply divide the number of items correct or students obtaining a specific score by the total number of items or students, and multiply by 100. For example, if 24 of 62 students obtain a passing score, it can be concluded that 39% of the students passed (24/62 × 100). Closely related to percentage is *proportion*, which expresses the result as part of one. Thus, in the previous example, the proportion of students passing is .39.

A *percentile* score or rank is a measure of relative standing, which indicates the percentage of scores in a distribution that are at or below a specified score. Hence, a score with a percentile rank of 70 is higher than 70% of the scores in the distribution. A percentile score is based on the number of items answered correctly, but it does not indicate the percentage of items answered correctly. In other words, a percentile score indicates the percentage of other scores that a student outscored. As we will see in Chapter 6, percentile scores are essential for interpreting norm-referenced tests.

Ranked (or rank-ordered) scores are those that are presented in order of magnitude (size) or frequency of scores. This indicates the relative position of each score or student. Consider the ranking of the following five scores from five students.

Score	Rank
90	1
85	2
83	3
81	4
70	5

Tied scores would yield the same rank for each score, determined by the average of the scores. Although ranking scores indicates relative position, it is a crude index of best to worst because the magnitude of the difference between the scores is not indicated. Ranked scores can under- or overestimate the degree of difference between scores. For example, if the difference between the grade point averages is small, such as a hundredth of a point separating the valedictorian and the other top four students in the class, it is reasonable to conclude that the difference between the students is, in a practical sense, meaningless. If the valedictorian scored a full three tenths higher than any other student, however, then the difference is significant. In both cases, a mere rank ordering, without consideration of the degree of difference, would have suggested that the differences between the rankings were the same.

In measurement, raw scores are often converted mathematically to other types of scores. This occurs with the SAT. Although each student answers a specific number of items correctly (raw score), what is reported is a *derived* score between 200 and 800. Of the several types of derived scores, some are considered in this chapter, and some are discussed in Chapter 6.

Frequency Distributions

When there are many scores or students, it would be difficult to understand and interpret the results as a whole without organizing the scores or students in a meaningful way. The *frequency distribution* is the most fundamental approach to organizing a set of data. This type of distribution simply indicates the number of students who obtained different scores. In a *simple frequency distribution*, the scores obtained are rank ordered from highest to lowest, and the number of students who obtained each score is tallied. Figure 5.1 shows how a group of scores can be represented by a simple frequency distribution. If there is a large number of scores or students, it may be best to use a *grouped frequency distribution*. In this type of distribution, score intervals are created, and the number of students whose scores are within each interval is indicated. This type of frequency distribution is also illustrated in Figure 5.1.

One disadvantage of grouped frequency distributions is that information about individual students may be lost. This problem is often encountered in summarizing a large number of scores. Although on the one hand, a single index or a few categories provide a more succinct summary, individual data are embedded within the group. To construct a group frequency distribution, determine the difference between the highest and lowest score and then divide that number by the number of intervals or categories desired. Usually, this is 5 to 10 intervals, although the actual number is determined somewhat arbitrarily. You will want to have a workable number of intervals and at the same time a sufficient number to reflect the variation in scores. In the end, you want intervals that provide the most accurate summary of the data in a condensed form. If possible, it is best to keep the size of the intervals the same.

		Simple Frequency Distribution		Grouped Frequency Distribution	
Student	Score	Score	f	Interval	f
Nina	98	98	1	92-98	3
Scott	94	94	2	86-91	3
Therease	94	92	1	80-85	5
Felix	88	88	1	74-79	5
Jim	86	86	2	70-73	4
Lex	86	85	1		
Jon	85	82	1		
Jan	82	80	3		
Hannah	80	79	1		
Karon	80	77	2		
Tyler	80	75	1		
Austin	79	74	1		
Tristen	77	72	2		
Megan	77	71	1		
Janine	75	70	1		
Freya	74				
Rosemary	72				
Frank	72				
Susan	71				
Benjamin	70				

Figure 5.1. Frequency Distributions of Test Scores

Shapes of Distributions

The shape of a distribution can tell a lot about the nature of the scores. When data are presented in the form of a list, such as in Figure 5.1, it is not easy to think of the overall distribution of scores as having a particular shape. To better understand shape, the data can be presented on a two-dimensional graph. The scores are placed, in ascending order from lowest to highest, on the horizontal part of the graph (x-axis), and values for the frequency with which each score was obtained are placed on the vertical part of the graph (y-axis). A *frequency polygon* is created when the graph is drawn to connect the frequencies of each score. A frequency polygon for the data in Figure 5.1 is illustrated in Figure 5.2.

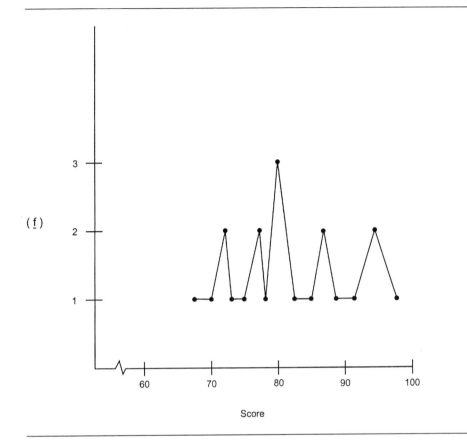

Figure 5.2. Frequency Polygon of Test Scores

With a large number of scores, the shape becomes smoother and is often referred to as a curve. Different types of curves provide generic information about the nature of the distribution. The most commonly used shape is the *normal curve* (Figure 5.3). The normal curve, a symmetrical, bell-shaped distribution, is important for two reasons. First, this distribution is found in nature when most traits or characteristics are measured, such as height, weight, size, temperature, wind velocity, intelligence, intensity, athletic prowess, and so on. Second, properties of the normal curve are used extensively in large-scale, standardized testing.

In a normal distribution, most of the scores cluster around the middle, with few at the highest and lowest ends. Because the normal curve is symmetrical, one side is a mirror image of the other side. That is, if the normal curve is divided down the middle, the halves are the same; one is a mirror image of the

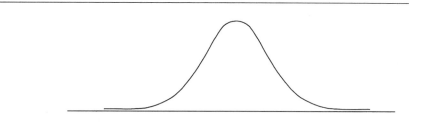

Figure 5.3. The Normal Distribution

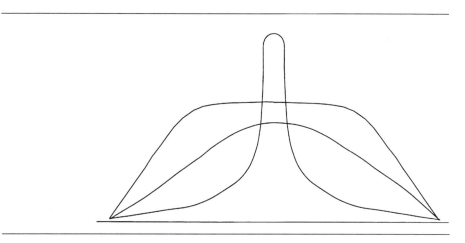

Figure 5.4. Symmetrical Distributions That Are Not Bell-Shaped

other. Being bell-shaped is also important. A symmetrical curve can be shaped in various ways, only one of which is bell-shaped (see Figure 5.4).

If a distribution is not symmetrical, then it may be characterized as *positively skewed, negatively skewed,* or *flat* (see Figure 5.5). In a positively skewed distribution, most of the scores piled up at the lower end, and there are just a few very high scores. This forms a tail that points in a positive direction, hence the name positive skew. Conversely, when there are mostly high scores with just a few low scores, the distribution is negatively skewed (tail points in a negative direction). In a flat, or rectangular, distribution, most of the scores have about the same frequency. Negatively skewed distributions are common in classroom assessments. In these tests, often most students do well, while just a few students do poorly.

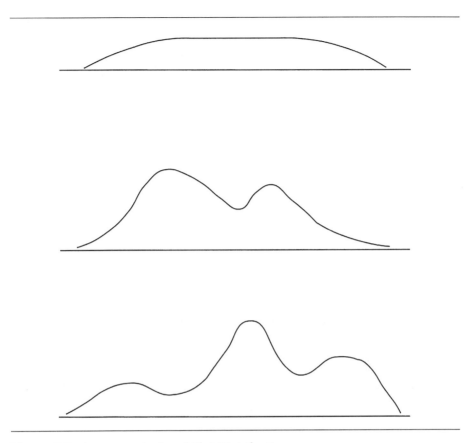

Figure 5.5. Asymmetrical and Flat Distributions

Measures of Central Tendency

Although frequency distributions and curves can show how scores are distributed, there is usually a need for even more succinct indexes that can capture the essence of the distribution. These indexes are called *measures of central tendency* because they are used to indicate, with a single number, the most typical or "average" score.

Mean

The *mean* is the arithmetic average. It is calculated by adding all the scores in the distribution and then dividing that sum by the number of scores. The mean is represented by $\overline{X}$ or *M*. For the set of scores in Figure 5.1, the mean is 81.

One drawback of the mean as a measure of the typical score is that it may be distorted with extremely high or low scores. Consider the following distributions and means. The distributions as a whole are the same with the exceptions of two scores. Yet this small difference results in vastly different means.

(1) 1, 2, 2, 3, 4, 4, 5, 5, 5, 6, 6, 8, 8, 8, 10   mean = 5.13
(2) 1, 2, 2, 3, 4, 4, 5, 5, 5, 6, 6, 8, 8, 80, 100   mean = 15.93

Because the mean is pulled in a positive direction in a distribution with a few atypical high scores, the distribution is positively skewed. It is as if the mean is skewed in a positive direction. The opposite is true for a distribution with a few very low scores that tend to skew the mean in a negative direction. This is what happens to students when a zero is averaged in as one of the scores in calculating interim or semester grades. The zero may distort the mean so much that it no longer indicates the typical performance of the student.

This principle is important whenever averages are used to describe a student, class, school, or school district. At the student level, many teachers average student test scores, quizzes, homework assignments, and other grades to determine a final 9-weeks or semester grade. This is typically done to obtain an overall percentage correct, which translates to a grade (e.g., 94-100 = A, 86-93 = B). Suppose you need to determine a final grade for Lakeith from the following products:

Homework	15 of 20 points
Quiz	22 of 25 correct
Quiz	24 of 25 correct
Paper	45 of 50 points
Final exam	78 of 100 points

The first step in combining these scores is to convert each to percentage correct:

Homework	75%
Quiz	88%
Quiz	96%
Paper	90%
Final exam	78%

If these percentages are averaged, the result is 85.4%. This approach has the effect of *weighting each of the five products the same.* That is, quizzes count twice as much as the final exam, and homework counts as much as the final exam. If you intend to weight each product differently, then each of the percentages needs to be multiplied by the appropriate weight, with each score added. For example, let's assume you want to use the following weights:

Homework	10%
Quiz	10%
Quiz	10%
Paper	20%
Final exam	50%

Multiplying each percentage correct score by the weight, then adding these numbers, gives a different result:

$$
\begin{aligned}
(75 \times .10) &= 7.5 \\
+ (88 \times .10) &= 8.8 \\
+ (96 \times .10) &= 9.6 \\
+ (90 \times .20) &= 18 \\
+ (78 \times .50) &= \underline{39} \\
& \quad\ \ 82.9
\end{aligned}
$$

Now let's see what happens if Lakeith misses a quiz and is given a zero, for both equal weighting and differential weighting:

Equal weighting: $(75\% + 88\% + 0\% + 90\% + 78\%)/5 = 66.2\%$

Differential weighting: $7.5 + 8.8 + 0 + 18 + 39 = 73.3$

These are obviously dramatic effects, and the more the zero is weighted, the more impact it will have on the average. Some contend that this type of averaging penalizes students for getting a zero. In a sense, this is true because averaging a zero with other scores literally weights it more because it is such an extreme score. As long as such an influential weight is understood, then the averaging process is not capricious.

Another use of the mean is to examine the overall performance of a class or school. Typically, a class or school average is computed and compared with other classes or schools and/or performance in earlier years. Important issues are involved when using the data in these ways. First, just as an extreme score can significantly affect the average for individual students, it also can affect the average for a class or school. This means that a few very low scores can skew the average for the entire class. Consequently, when analyzing scores for the class as a whole, it is prudent to examine the frequency distribution along with the mean. This will show extreme scores and clusters of scores that will help make interpretations more accurate.

Second, teachers find class averages most useful when the data are reported for subgroups of students and knowledge or skills. The mean score for students in a class who have demonstrated very high achievement in previous quizzes, homework, in-class worksheets, and other assignments should be higher than the mean score of students who have struggled with the content. This type of report helps validate the interpretation that high scores indeed suggest high achievement. By breaking an overall mean into subscales or parts, the teacher is able to use these results in a diagnostic way to identify areas that may need further instruction or even remediation.

Third, comparing mean scores with the scores of students from previous years or with students from other schools requires care because although the scores are based on the same test, there are invariably differences in other factors that affect the average score, such as ability levels of students, motivation, and administration procedures. For example, in one school, all students may take the test, whereas in another school, students whose primary language is not English are exempted. For a variety of reasons, students as a group change from year to year, so even longitudinal data from the same school can be misleading if these differences are not taken into account in interpreting the averages.

Median and Mode

The *median* is the midpoint or middle point of the distribution. In other words, the median is the value of the score that has 50% of the scores below it and 50% of the scores above it. Thus, the median is the score that is at the 50th percentile. The median is found by rank ordering every score in the distribution, including each score that is the same, and locating the score that has half of the scores above it and half below it. For the distribution in Figure 5.1, the median is 80 (in distributions that have an even number of scores, the median is the sum of the two middle scores divided by 2). The median is not distorted by extreme low or high scores and is a better indication of typical score in skewed distributions than the mean.

The *mode* is simply the score that occurs most frequently. In the distribution in Figure 5.1, more students scored an 80 (3) than any other score, so the mode is 80. In some distributions, there can be more than a single mode. For example, if two scores occur the same and both are the highest frequency scores, the distribution is *bimodal.*

In a normal distribution, the mean, median, and mode are the same. In a positively skewed distribution, the mean is greater than the median and mode, whereas in a negatively skewed distribution, the mean is less than the

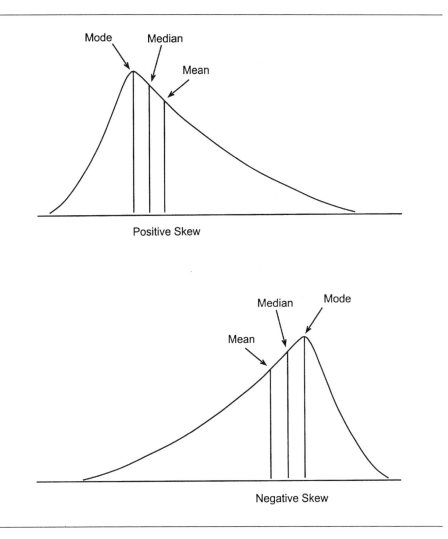

Figure 5.6. Mean, Median, and Mode in Skewed Distributions

median and mode. The relationship between the three measures of central tendency are illustrated in skewed distributions in Figure 5.6.

Measures of Dispersion

Although a measure of central tendency is a good indicator of the most typical score in a distribution, it is also useful to know something about how much the scores cluster around the mean or median. Statistics that show how much the scores spread out from the mean are called measures of *dispersion* or mea-

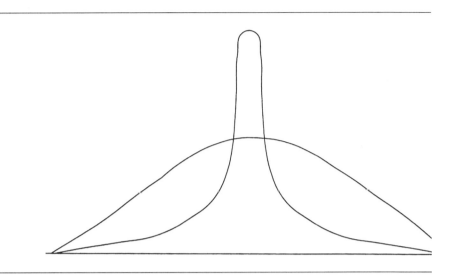

Figure 5.7. Distributions With Different Dispersion

sures of *variability*. If the scores are highly dispersed, different, scattered, spread, or dissimilar, then the distribution is characterized as having high *variability* or *variance*. That is, the scores vary considerably. If the scores are bunched together close to the mean, then there is little dispersion and low variability or small variance.

The need for a measure of dispersion to describe a distribution is illustrated in Figure 5.7. These two distributions have the same mean, median, and mode but portray different groups of scores. A complete description is possible only if a measure of dispersion is included.

Although it is sometimes helpful to use general terms such as *small, large, great, little,* and *high* to describe the amount of dispersion in the distribution, three measures are typically used to more specifically indicate variance: range, interquartile range, and standard deviation.

Range and Interquartile Range

The *range* is simply the numerical difference between the highest and lowest scores in the distribution. It is calculated by subtracting the lowest score from the highest score. The range is a crude measure of dispersion because it is based on only two scores from the distribution, and it does not indicate anything about relative cluster of scores. In a highly skewed distribution, the range is particularly misleading, suggesting a higher degree of dispersion than actually exists.

The *interquartile range* indicates the middle 50% of the scores in the distribution. By limiting the measure to the middle 50% of the scores, the major-

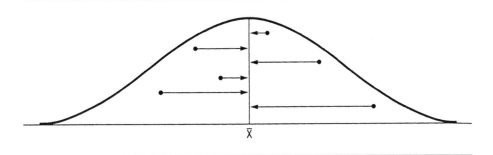

Figure 5.8. Illustration of Distance of Each Score From the Mean

SOURCE = Reprinted from *Research in Education: A Conceptual Introduction*, p. 218, by J. H. McMillan and S. Schumacher, 1997 (4th ed.), New York: Addison Wesley/Longman. Copyright © 1997 by Addison Wesley Educational Publishers, Inc. Reprinted by permission of Addison Wesley Educational Publishers, Inc.

ity of the scores are included in the calculation of dispersion, but extreme high or low scores that would influence the range are excluded. The interquartile range is determined by subtracting the score at the 25th percentile from the score at the 75th percentile. In the distribution in Figure 5.1, the interquartile range is 13 (87 – 74).

Standard Deviation

A more complicated but more informative and precise measure of dispersion is *standard deviation*, a number that indicates the average distance of the scores from the mean. It tells, in other words, how far most scores are from the mean. A distribution that has scores that are bunched together close to the mean will have a small standard deviation, whereas distributions with scores spread way out from the mean will have a large standard deviation.

Standard deviation is calculated with what may look like a complicated formula, but the steps are relatively easy to follow:

1. Calculate the mean of the distribution.
2. Calculate the difference each score is from the mean (see Figure 5.8).
3. Square each difference score.
4. Add the squared difference scores.
5. Divide by the total number of scores in the distribution.
6. Calculate the square root.

These six steps are illustrated in Figure 5.9 with the scores from Figure 5.1.

(1)	(2)	(3) Deviation Score Squared	(4) Squared Deviation Score Added	(5) Added Scores Divided by N	(6)
Calculate the Mean	Deviation Score				Square Root
98	98 − 81 = 17	289	289		
94	94 − 81 = 13	169	+169		
94	94 − 81 = 13	169	+169		
88	88 − 81 = 7	49	+49		
86	86 − 81 = 5	25	+25		
86	86 − 81 = 5	25	+25		
85	85 − 81 = 4	16	+16		
82	82 − 81 = 1	1	+1		
80	80 − 81 = −1	1	+1		
80	80 − 81 = −1	1	+1		
80	80 − 81 = −1	1	+1		
79	79 − 81 = −2	4	+4		
77	77 − 81 = −4	16	+16		
77	77 − 81 = −4	16	+16		
75	75 − 81 = −6	36	+36		
74	74 − 81 = −7	49	+49		
72	72 − 81 = −9	81	+81		
72	72 − 81 = −9	81	+81		
71	71 − 81 = −10	100	+100		
70	70 − 81 = −11	121	+121		
1620/20 = 81			1250	1250/20 = 62.5	$\sqrt{62.5} = 7.9$

Figure 5.9. Steps in Calculating Standard Deviation

Essentially, standard deviation is finding how much each score differs from the mean and then finding the average difference score, or, in other words, finding the average distance of the scores from the mean. Simply calculate the squared deviation scores, find the average deviation score, and then take the square root to return to the original unit of measurement. The most common convention in reporting and using standard deviation is to indicate that one standard deviation is equal to some number (e.g., 1 SD = 5). In a normal distribution, there are certain properties to standard deviation that are universal and that help in understanding the scores. The meaning of "one standard deviation" is always the same in a normal distribution, regardless of the unit of standard deviation. For instance, a score in a normal distribution that is at +1 standard deviation will be at the 84th percentile. This is true for any normal distribution. If one distribution has a mean of 40 and a standard

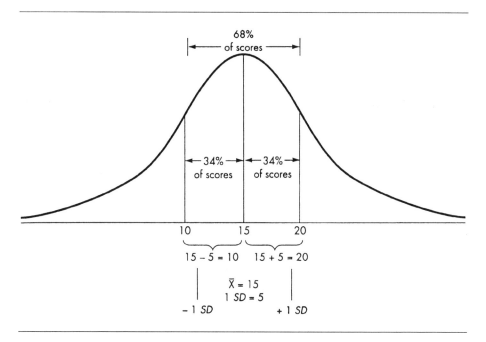

Figure 5.10. Relation of Standard Deviation to Percentile Rank

SOURCE: Reprinted from *Research in Education: A Conceptual Introduction*, p. 219, by J. H. McMillan and S. Schumacher, 1997 (4th ed.), New York: Addison Wesley/Longman. Copyright © 1997 by Addison Wesley Educational Publishers, Inc. Reprinted by permission of Addison Wesley Educational Publishers, Inc.

deviation of 5, a score of 45 is at the same percentile as a score of 6.5 in a distribution that has a mean of 6 and a standard deviation of 0.5.

Because the normal curve is symmetrical, it can describe the approximate percentage of scores that are contained within given units of standard deviation. This is illustrated in Figure 5.10, where 1 *SD* = 5. On both sides of the mean (15), there is a line that designates -1 and +1 *SD*. The negative and positive directions from the mean are equivalent in score units. That is, both -1 and +1 *SD* are 5 score units. Between -1 and +1 *SD* is about 68% of the total number of scores in the distribution. This is determined by knowing that if the mean is the 50th percentile, which it is for a normal distribution, and +1 *SD* is at the 84th percentile, then subtracting 50 from 84 shows that 34% of the scores in the distribution must be between the mean and +1 *SD*. Because the distribution is symmetrical, the same is true for the percentage of scores between the mean and -1 *SD* (34%). Thus, adding 34% and 34% yields a total of 68% of the scores of the distribution within one standard deviation of the mean.

Figure 5.11 shows a more complete description of the normal curve and units of standard deviation. As long as the distribution is normal, +2 *SD* will be at the 98th percentile, and -2 *SD* will be at the 2nd percentile. In other words, if

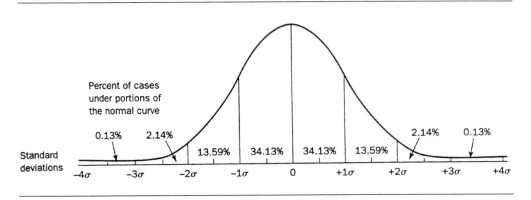

Figure 5.11. Normal Probability Curve

SOURCE: Reprinted from "Methods of Expressing Test Scores," by H. G. Seashore, in *Test Service Notebook No. 148*, September 1980, of The Psychological Corporation, a Harcourt Assessment Company. Copyright © 1980. Reprinted with permission.

a student's score is at two standard deviations above the mean, the student did better than 98% of the other scores in the distribution. In a normal distribution, 96% of the scores are between +2 and -2 *SD*.

Correlation

Correlation was introduced in Chapter 2. Here, I will examine this important descriptive statistic in more detail, as well as how correlations are represented graphically and properly interpreted.

Correlation Coefficients

A correlation measures the degree to which the scores of two or more variables or factors are related. The *correlation coefficient* (r) is a number between -1 and +1 that is calculated to indicate the strength and direction of the relationship. A correlation coefficient is calculated by a formula and is reported as r = .76, r = -.35, r = .04, and so on (notice that there is a minus sign before a negative correlation but no plus sign in front of a positive correlation). Although there are a number of types of correlation coefficients, the one encountered most in assessment is called the Pearson product-moment correlation. A positive correlation means that as the value of one variable increases, so does the value of the other variable. This is also called a *direct* relationship. If the correlation coefficient is between 0 and +1, it is positive. A negative or inverse corre-

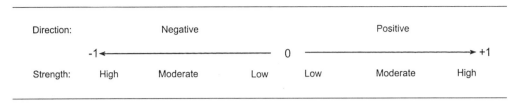

Figure 5.12. Relationship of Strength and Direction of Correlation

lation is indicated by a negative coefficient and indicates that as the value of one variable increases, the value of the other variable decreases. A negative or inverse correlation is represented by a number between 0 and -1.

A positive correlation is not necessarily any better than a negative one. For example, a desirable positive correlation exists between time spent studying and achievement, whereas an undesirable positive correlation would be student anxiety and referrals to the counselor's office. Conversely, there are many helpful negative relationships, such as those between student attention and teacher rebukes, or time teachers lecture and student attitudes. An undesirable negative correlation would be student disruptions and student achievement.

The coefficient also indicates the strength or magnitude of the relationship, independent of direction. Strength refers to the degree of the relationship, that is, how powerful or helpful it is in predicting one variable from another. A high positive value (e.g., $r = .93$, $r = .85$, or $r = .88$) represents a high or strong positive relationship (+1 is a perfect relationship). The same is true for a high negative value ($r = -.93$, $r = -.85$, or $r = -.88$). A low value, those close to zero, indicate a weak or small relationship, whereas values midway between 0 and +1 or -1 indicate moderate relationships (e.g., $r = -.45$, $r = .62$). Thus, the strength of the relationship becomes stronger as the correlation coefficient approaches either +1 or -1 from 0. This is illustrated in Figure 5.12.

Scatterplots

Although the correlation coefficient is used extensively to report relationships, the scatterplot or scatter diagram is needed to interpret the coefficient correctly. The scatterplot is a graphic representation of the relationship. It is formed by making a visual array of the intersection of each student's scores on the two variables or measures. The two-dimensional graph is made by rank ordering the values of one variable on the horizontal axis, from low to high, and rank ordering the values of the second variable on the vertical axis. For example, to correlate student achievement scores with self-concept scores, the range of results for the achievement scores could be placed on the horizontal axis and range of self-concept results on the vertical axis. This relationship is

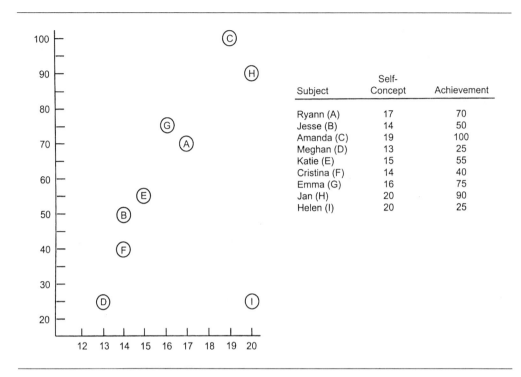

Figure 5.13. Scatterplot of Achievement Related to Self-Concept

illustrated in Figure 5.13 with a few students. The student scores are summarized next to the graph in random order. The intersections of each set of scores
is indicated in the graph with the letters. Together, these intersection points
form a pattern that provides a general indication of the relationship. Figure
5.13 shows a positive relationship. As achievement scores increase, self-
concept scores increase.

The scatterplot is helpful in identifying two aspects of correlation that affect the interpretation of the coefficient. The first is to determine if there are
any atypical scores as related to the overall pattern. In the illustration in Figure
5.13, for instance, the intersection of Helen's scores is not at all consistent with
the pattern. This atypical score, or *outlier*, reduces or lowers the coefficient to
give the impression of less relationship than actually exists. It is similar to the
effect that an extreme score has on the mean. In this case, there is a *spurious*
correlation, rather than a *skewed* distribution.

The general pattern also indicates if the relationship is linear or curvilinear. The Pearson product-moment correlation coefficient is calculated as if
the relationship is a linear one. Thus, if the scatterplot identifies a curvilinear
pattern, then the coefficient will be lower than the actual relationship.

Interpreting Correlations

Because correlations are used extensively in assessment, it is important to interpret the meaning of correlation coefficients accurately. There are three primary limitations to consider: correlation and causation, restricted range, and the size of coefficients.

Correlation and Causation

It is tempting to think that a correlation describes a cause-and-effect relationship, but that is rarely the case. An accurate interpretation of a correlation *always* begins with the understanding that the relationship is descriptive only of a predictive relationship—that to some degree, the value of one variable or measure can be predicted from knowledge of value of another one. You should not conclude that one variable *caused* the change in the other or was the *reason* that the values of the other measure or variable changed.

Correlation does not imply causation for two reasons. First, a relationship between A and B may be high, but there is no way to know if A caused B or B caused A. For example, consider the relationship between achievement and self-concept illustrated in Figure 5.13. Although it is clearly positive, we don't know if achievement affects self-concept, or if self-concept influences achievement. That is, it would be incorrect to conclude that programs are needed to enhance self-concept, thinking that this would increase achievement. Second, there may also be variables that are unaccounted for that explain the relationship. Think about the relationship between spending per pupil and achievement. If it is positive, does it mean that increased funding will increase achievement? Perhaps, but many other variables associated with family background and SES, such as parental education, income, and community attitudes, are probably more responsible for achievement. Just pouring more money in the schools would not raise achievement much because of the strong effect of these family and community factors. In Figure 5.14, I have illustrated the principle of additional variables by showing a strong positive relationship between body weight and reading comprehension. Hard to believe? When you follow the steps in Figure 5.14, you see that a positive relationship is built by stringing together a series of near-zero correlations. How? A third variable, age, is related to weight, and obviously there is a positive relationship between age and reading comprehension.

Despite these two limitations, correlations are still misinterpreted to mean something causal—perhaps because it seems so reasonable, given the language that is used. For example, when there is a positive correlation between time on task and achievement, it seems obvious that increasing time on task will increase achievement, and in fact, this might be true. It simply

1. Plot the body weight and scores of a group of first graders:

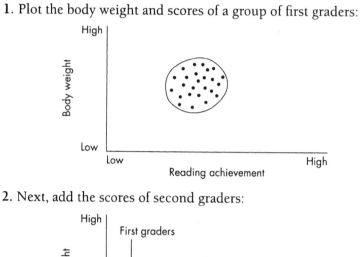

2. Next, add the scores of second graders:

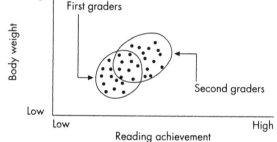

3. Finally, add the scores of pupils in grades three through six:

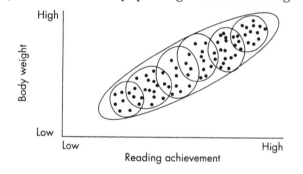

Figure 5.14. Correlation Between Weight and Reading Comprehension

sounds logical, like the positive correlation between amount of rain and growth of crops. But do not be lulled into thinking that the reason or cause of increases in achievement is an increase in time on task. The reality is that we don't know if increased achievement caused students to be on task more, or if other unaccounted-for variables are actually responsible for the increases.

Maybe students were given different incentives along with more study time, or maybe the increased time on task consisted of one-on-one tutoring. There are many other possible causal explanations, which if left unaccounted for, necessitate great caution in concluding that in this case, achievement increased *because* of more time on task.

Restricted Range

A second limitation in interpreting correlation is that some correlations may underestimate the true value of the relationship because the variability of one of the measures or factors is not as high as it should be or could be. That is, if the range of scores for one of the variables is confined to only a part of the total distribution, the correlation will be lowered. This is called *restriction in range.* Suppose, for example, you want to examine the relationship between grade point average and standardized test scores of gifted students. Because the range of grades and test scores of these students is restricted, the correlation would probably be small. Restriction in range is one reason why modest relationships, at best, are reported between college entrance exams, such as the SAT, and achievement in college. The range of test scores is limited to students who scored relatively high.

Size of the Correlation Coefficient

The third limitation to consider is concerned with the size of the correlation coefficient. There is a convention that a high number is described as a strong relationship, but this gives only a hint of the true or actual magnitude of the relationship. This is because it is easy to think of the decimal as a percentage, so that a correlation of .70 means 70% of 100% of the possible relationship. Actually, the amount of the relationship that is common among the two measures or variables is estimated by squaring the correlation and thinking of that as a percentage. Thus, .70 squared is .49, or 49%. This has a dramatic impact on what the correlation means because as the correlation lessens, the amount of relationship in common is reduced exponentially ($r = .50, 25\%$; $r = .30, 9\%$). This squared value (called the *coefficient of determination*) is the more accurate indicator of the magnitude of the relationship.

Another consideration related to the size of the correlations is that many will be labeled *significant* although they are small and account for a very small amount of common variance (e.g., $r = .20, 4\%$). Researchers use the term *significant* in this context to mean that the correlation is statistically different from no relationship at all. It is quite possible, especially in studies that have a large number of participants, that a small correlation will be reported as statistically significant. This does *not*, however, mean that the correlation is important or meaningful.

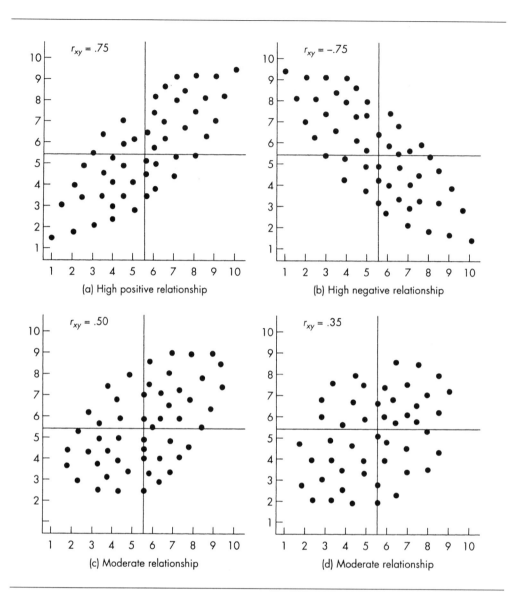

Figure 5.15. Scatterplots of Different Correlations

SOURCE: Reprinted from *Using Standardized Tests in Education*, p. 49, by W. A. Mehrens and I. J. Lehmann, 1987, 4th ed., White Plains, NY: Longman. Copyright © by W. A. Mehrens. Used by permission of W. A. Mehrens.

The importance of the size of correlations is illustrated further in Figure 5.15, which shows scatterplots of four correlations. Take a score of 5.5 on the horizontal axis and look at the range of scores it predicts on the second variable. For scatterplot (a), which is a relatively high correlation, predicted scores range from 3 to 8. This is not as precise as the .75 correlation might seem to imply.

Using Data to Improve Assessments

One of the helpful uses of descriptive data is to use summary statistics about individual items to improve assessments. With traditional selected-response tests, the first item statistic of interest is the difficulty of each item. *Difficulty* is simply the percentage of students who answered the item correctly. A difficult item may be answered by fewer than half the students, whereas an easy item may be answered correctly by all students. If the purpose of the test is to provide a norm-referenced interpretation, difficulty values around 50% are desirable. The difficulty index, then, informs about which items are helping to discern a difference between students in what they know and can do.

In most classroom tests, however, the interpretation is criterion referenced. The typical difficulty index for items will usually vary between 60% and 100%. For items that are answered correctly by only a few students, review the items to determine if the scores are low because the item was poor, because instruction was inappropriate for the items, or because students in fact do not understand what is being assessed. For items that are answered correctly by all students, review the items to see if there are flaws in the items that result in correct answers even by students who do not have the knowledge and skills that are being assessed. Another way to check these items is to use them before and then after instruction in a pretest-posttest design. If students are unable to answer the item correctly prior to instruction and then know the answer after instruction, then the item is working well to document student learning. For items answered correctly by some students, check to see if the students who answered correctly did well on other, related work and whether students who did not know the answer did poorly on related work. If both of these conditions are present, then the item is a good one.

A second procedure to use with items that are used for norm-referenced interpretations is to calculate the *discriminating power* of the item. The discriminating power of an item refers to the ability of the item to discriminate between students whose total score is high and students whose total score is low. A discrimination index for each item can be calculated by completing five steps:

1. Rank order all students on the basis of total score.
2. Divide the scores into a high and a low group (usually the top quarter or third and bottom quarter or third).
3. Tally the number of students who obtained the correct answer in each group.
4. Subtract the number of correct answers in the low group from the number of correct answers in the high group.
5. Divide the difference by the total number of student scores in the high-scoring and low-scoring groups divided by 2.

Table 5.1 Summary of Student Scores on Three Assessments

	Test A			Test B			Giving a Speech		
	Total	Item		Total	Item		Total	Eye	Voice
Student	Score	1	2	Score	1	2	Rating	Contact	Clarity
George	70	w	w	24	r	r	5	5	2
Ron	60	r	w	30	r	w	5	4	3
Sally	75	r	r	28	w	r	3	2	3
Tamika	83	r	w	19	w	w	4	4	1
Mica	72	w	w	24	r	r	2	1	4
Helen	88	r	r	22	r	r	2	2	3
Rosemary	85	r	w	18	w	w	4	3	5
Ashley	78	w	w	27	w	r	4	2	5
Kenya	92	r	r	29	r	w	5	5	5

A positive discrimination index of .40 or better suggests that the item is doing a good job of separating students on the basis of what they know. Any negative discrimination index means that the item is working against the purpose of the test. Such items need to be reviewed carefully. For example, suppose a class of 20 students takes a test. Three of the top five scoring students answered question 3 correctly, while four of the bottom five students obtained the right answer. The discrimination index of this item is -.20: $(3 - 4)/5$.

Discriminating power is not as useful with criterion-referenced interpretations or with performance assessments because the range of performance is smaller, and, with performance assessments, there are few tasks (items). If the assessment is structured to provide different levels of competence, something more than simply pass/fail, then the items can be analyzed to see if they discriminate on the basis of categorizing students in one of the levels. That is, if all students categorized as "exemplary" answer an item correctly, and students designated as "fail to understand" miss the item, then the item is discriminating as needed. In a performance assessment, the same logic can be used as long as a sufficient number of tasks are evaluated. Each task is like an item.

To apply these principles, a record of the performance of nine students on three assessments is summarized in Table 5.1. Use the principles of difficulty and discrimination to answer the following questions:

1. What is the difficulty index for each item?

2. What is the discrimination index for each item?

3. Are eye contact and voice clarity (two of many rating categories) contributing appropriately to the total rating on "Giving a Speech"?

Answers to these questions are found at the end of this chapter.

Answers to Difficulty and Discrimination Index Questions

1. What is the difficulty index for each item?

   Test A, Item 1: 67%   Test A, Item 2: 33%

   Test B, Item 1: 56%   Test B, Item 2: 56%

2. What is the discrimination index for each item?

   Test A, Item 1: .67   Test A, Item 2: .67

   Test B, Item 1: .33   Test B, Item 2: 0

3. Are eye contact and voice clarity contributing appropriately to the total rating on "Giving a Speech"?

   Eye contact: The three highest-rated students had an eye contact average score of 4.7. The three lowest-rated students had an average eye contact score of 1.7. Yes, eye contact is contributing as appropriate.

   Voice clarity: The three highest-rated students had a voice clarity rating of 3.3. The three lowest-rated students had an average clarity rating of 3.3. Because the average clarity ratings of the students are the same, the voice clarity ratings are not working as appropriate.

Although data from assessment results can be used to better understand student learning, as well as to improve subsequent assessments, such analysis should always be tempered with professional judgment. Descriptive data are useful, but more as a general indicator than a precise measure that drives specific conclusions or practice. Data must be judged on validity, reliability, and fairness, along with other factors that influence interpretation or use. In other words, the descriptive data from assessments are only some of many considerations in making implications and drawing conclusions.

CHAPTER 6

Interpreting and Using National and State Standardized Assessments

A growing trend in education is the use of large-scale, standardized student assessments at the national and state level. These assessments are used for a variety of purposes:

- To identify students who may be eligible to receive special services
- To monitor student performance through time
- To identify students' academic strengths and weaknesses
- To predict performance
- To determine readiness for new academic work
- To select students for special programs
- To improve teaching
- To evaluate programs
- To give feedback to students and parents
- To compare schools and students
- To evaluate curriculum
- To determine if performance standards for grade promotion and graduation have been demonstrated
- To evaluate teachers
- To evaluate principals
- To evaluate and accredit schools

Some of these purposes, such as monitoring student performance through time and predicting performance, have been used to justify the ad-

Table 6.1 Ways of Classifying Characteristics of Standardized Assessments

Function	Scope	Interpretation	Level	Publisher
Achievement	National	Norm-referenced	Individual	Federal government
Aptitude	State	Criterion-referenced	Group	Commercial
	District			State
				District

ministration and reporting of standardized aptitude and achievement tests for decades. In recent years, use of large-scale assessment for the last four purposes listed above has accelerated and intensified (Heubert & Hauser, 1999; Phelps, 1998). When standardized assessments, whether at the state, local, or national level, are used to deny students promotion in grade or graduation, to evaluate school personnel, or to accredit schools, the results of the assessments have serious implications. Assessments used for these purposes are called "high-stakes" assessments (of course, it is not the assessments that are high stakes, but the way the results are used). Because high-stakes assessments are commonly employed at all levels, it is imperative to understand appropriate uses and limitations when interpreting the scores.

This chapter will first examine different types of standardized assessments and how they are administered and prepared for. I will also review the nature of the scores that are reported and how to interpret them. Finally, this chapter will look at how standardized test scores can be used to improve instruction.

Types of Standardized Assessments

Recall that an assessment is standardized if there are established, "standard" procedures for administration, scoring, and reporting of results. Beyond these general criteria, however, there are many variations or types of standardized assessments. Table 6.1 summarizes five ways of classifying standardized assessments. Each of these categories describes characteristics that influence the makeup of the assessment and the way results are reported and interpreted. With some exceptions, the categories are independent of one another. For example, a test that is national in scope could serve an achievement or aptitude function, use norm- or criterion-referenced interpretations, and be administered individually or to groups of students. The most important difference in standardized assessments is in function. Let's consider in further detail the nature of assessments that are typical in each of these two major types.

Standardized Achievement Assessments: What Do Students Know?

Standardized achievement assessments (standardized tests) have been a mainstay of American education for decades. The purpose of these tests is to measure how much students have learned in specific, well-defined content areas such as reading, mathematics, science, social science, and English. The tests are typically published by companies for profit, for use throughout the country. This has some important implications. Because the tests need to appeal to a broad spectrum of potential users, the material that is covered is common to most school districts. The advantage of broad coverage is that these tests measure outcomes and content that are shared by most schools in the nation. This allows significant comparisons with the achievement of other students throughout the country. A disadvantage of such broad coverage of content, however, is that there may not be a good match between the test and the local curriculum. Close inspection of the test objectives and types of items is needed to determine the extent of the match.

Increasingly, standardized achievement tests have been developed at the state and district level in response to the need for greater accountability. In contrast to national achievement tests, however, which tend to be norm referenced, state and district standardized tests are usually criterion referenced. The purpose of these state and district tests is typically related to specific learning outcomes, rather than to the broader skills and knowledge tapped by national norm-referenced tests. The results of the state and district tests often have direct consequences for students and schools. For students, specified levels of performance may be required to graduate from high school or even be promoted to the next grade. School accreditation may depend on students' obtaining certain scores. For example, in Virginia, a state testing program has been implemented for students in grades 3, 5, 8, and in high school (in various subjects). For a school to be fully accredited, at least 70% of the students must pass the tests that are administered (except 50% in grades 3 and 5 in science and social studies).

The most common type of national norm-referenced standardized test is the *survey battery,* which consists of a comprehensive set of subject matter tests, all normed on the same group. This type of norming allows comparisons between the subject matter areas tested to help determine students' relative strengths and weaknesses. That is, it can be determined that a student is strong in computational skills and weak in reading comprehension. It is not possible to make such determinations from different tests. Common norm-referenced standardized achievement survey batteries include the following:

- California Achievement Tests
- *TerraNova* Comprehensive Tests of Basic Skills
- Iowa Test of Basic Skills

- Metropolitan Achievement Tests
- Stanford Achievement Test Series (Stanford 9)

In addition to providing survey batteries, publishing companies also develop tests in specific subjects, such as mathematics and reading. These tests cover a content area with greater depth and breadth. Although a subject-specific test uses the same types of items as a survey battery, there are many more questions on each subject than are found on a survey battery, which allows greater specification of strengths and weaknesses within a subject. Often, these tests are used as a follow-up to a survey battery that may have identified possible difficulties. Reading tests, for example, are used extensively to focus on a number of specific reading skills. Thus, although a survey battery may provide scores in language, reading comprehension, and vocabulary, a subject-specific reading test may examine students' decoding skills, their ability to identify the main idea in a passage, and their ability to use context to understand the meaning of words.

The primary purpose of achievement test batteries is to survey student learning and obtain an overall performance score for each content area and major categories within each content area. Because the results are general, they do not provide to teachers much information that is helpful for instruction. To address this limitation, test publishers have developed *diagnostic batteries* for the major content areas. Diagnostic batteries, typically given in mathematics, reading, and language, provide criterion-referenced interpretations to identify a student's specific strengths and weaknesses in a particular subject. These results help teachers make instructional decisions such as whether students need remediation. For example, the Metropolitan Achievement Test series includes a norm-referenced reading survey test and a criterion-referenced reading diagnostic test. The diagnostic test provides scores in the following areas:

- Visual discrimination
- Letter recognition
- Auditory discrimination
- Sight vocabulary
- Phoneme/grapheme: consonants
- Phoneme/grapheme: vowels
- Vocabulary in context
- Word part clues
- Rate of comprehension
- Skimming and scanning
- Reading comprehension

As the nature of the list indicates, the diagnostic scores focus on areas that parallel instruction. Many testing companies offer tailor-made criterion-referenced diagnostic tests for states or districts. The state or district selects the objectives it wants measured from a large bank of objectives provided by the publisher. Items measuring the objectives are then pulled from a large bank of items provided by the publisher. For example, the Multiscore System has more than 1,500 objectives and 5,500 test items.

Some achievement batteries attempt to serve both survey and diagnostic purposes. This is accomplished by giving a score in major categories and then breaking down student performance on specific items corresponding to the diagnostic information that is useful for instruction. Because there are only a few items in each area, however, be wary of claims that the test can be both norm-referenced and criterion-referenced. In general, a minimum of 6 to 10 items is needed to make a reliable interpretation of the student's skill level or knowledge. Yet some test reports will contain 3 or 4 items for a specific area or skill, indicate how many were answered correctly, and then provide a judgment about competence. These summaries can provide an initial indication of achievement, but there needs to be further assessment to be sure about the student's strengths and weaknesses. Remember, test publishers want to sell as many tests as possible, so they do whatever they can to appeal to potential buyers who want a test that serves both norm-referenced and criterion-referenced purposes. Survey battery norm-referenced interpretations are better than survey criterion-referenced interpretations.

The federal government is involved in standardized testing through the National Assessment of Educational Progress (NAEP). The NAEP includes a series of achievement tests that has periodically, since 1969, measured the knowledge and skills of students aged 9, 13, and 17, and at various grade levels. Subject areas assessed have included reading, writing, mathematics, science, citizenship, history, art, social studies, and additional subjects. Performance data are reported for the nation and for various subgroups categorized by region, gender, race/ethnicity, parental education, type of school, and type and size of community. Instructional practices are also surveyed and related to the achievement scores. Samples are selected carefully for each administration to allow longitudinal analyses of the results. This provides one of the few national student achievement indicators that can pinpoint progress toward increasing performance through many years. Current NAEP data are reported as scale scores (0 to 500) and according to the percentage of students placed in one of three reporting categories: basic, proficient, and advanced. For example, the 1998 NAEP reading assessment compared 1998 scores with those in 1992 and 1994. Average reading scores increased for students in grades 4, 8, and 12. The percentages of students performing at or above the basic level of reading achievement were 62%, 74%, and 77%, respectively (National Assessment of Educational Progress, 1999). This is a criterion-referenced interpretation. In mathematics, there are five proficiency levels:

- Simple arithmetic facts

- Beginning skills and understanding

- Basic operations and beginning problem solving

- Moderately complex procedures and reasoning

- Multistep problem solving and algebra

The NAEP has become a visible way to provide a national report card on student achievement. It is frequently cited as evidence that schools are not measuring up. More information on NAEP can be obtained from its Web site on the Internet (*http://nces.ed.gov/naep*). NAEP data provide a wealth of information, and, because NAEP is now more accessible at the state and district level, the results can be used as another source of evidence of student performance, complementing standardized survey batteries and single-subject tests.

Standardized Aptitude Assessments

Standardized aptitude assessments measure a student's cognitive ability, potential, or capacity to learn. The purpose of these tests is to predict future performance or behavior. The aptitude that is measured is determined by both in-school and out-of-school experiences. This is how these tests differ from achievement tests. By including more out-of-school experiences, a broader set of skills is measured. But the difference between standardized achievement and aptitude tests is one of degree. There is considerable overlap in what is covered, and often the same or similar items are used in both types.

Aptitude tests are developed to enable prediction of future performance by assessing current general ability (not innate capacity that cannot change). An understanding of the general ability level of students is helpful in designing appropriate instruction and grouping of students. Suppose one class, overall, has a low ability level, and another class has a high ability level. Would it make sense to use the same instructional approach and materials for both classes? Would it be reasonable to give the same homework assignments to each class?

An important aspect of standardized aptitude assessments is the nature of the theory that is used as a basis for defining *aptitude*. Many theories can be used, each of which results in a unique conceptualization and interpretation. For many years, aptitude tests were designed to assess general cognitive ability, or intelligence. More recently, two trends have emerged. First, the language associated with aptitude tests has changed. It is now common to call these assessments *ability* tests (e.g., school ability, cognitive ability, or learning ability), despite little change in the nature of the initial aptitude tests. This change in language implies that *ability* communicates both innate and experiential influences, whereas *intelligence* tends to put the focus on innate, in-herited characteristics.

Second, theories of aptitude have changed considerably in the last two decades, stressing new capabilities and conceptualizations. Although early ap-titude tests, such as the Stanford-Binet, were based on Binet's theory of intelli-gence, Charles Spearman's development of g (general factor) and specific fac-tors, and Thurstone's primary mental abilities theory, later developments by Robert Sternberg (1985) and Howard Gardner (1993) have offered new insights into the nature of aptitudes. Gardner, for example, postulates that there are *multiple intelligences,* including musical, interpersonal, bodily/kinesthetic, linguistic, and intrapersonal. Sternberg's triarchic theory of intelligence in-cludes the internal world of the individual (further divided into metacompon-ents, performance components, and knowledge-acquisition components), ex-periences of the individual, and external contextual abilities as three aspects of intellectual functioning. These new conceptualizations imply that although there is undoubtedly a general ability for abstract thinking, evidence for valid-ity needs to be grounded in appropriate theory that may measure more spe-cific capabilities that are relevant for predicting performance.

Group Aptitude Assessments

Most aptitude assessments administered in schools are group tests, in which students respond to written questions at one time together. The items are usually multiple-choice to allow for efficient machine scoring. Three widely used group aptitude assessments are the Test of Cognitive Skills, the Otis-Lennon School Ability Test, and the Cognitive Abilities Test. The Cognitive Abilities Test for grades 3 through 12 (Multilevel Edition) is a good example of the types of aptitudes that are measured by group aptitude assessments. There are nine subtests, grouped into three categories (verbal, nonverbal, and quantitative) that are used for reporting the results. There is also an overall, or *composite,* score, but no scores for the nine subtests. Examples of the types of items found in these subtests are illustrated in Figure 6.1. Both the verbal and quantitative areas stress skills that are not directly taught in school, but the items require the use of skills that are learned in and outside school. The non-verbal section focuses on reasoning skills and is a good measure of reasoning abilities for language deficient students or poor readers. These examples are provided because it is important to understand the nature of the performance demanded by the items. What is termed "verbal" in one test may be different from "verbal" in another test.

Group aptitude tests are used primarily as screening devices. They are de-signed to identify students whose abilities deviate substantially from the norm. Individual assessment is typically carried out for students with sus-pected deficiencies.

Battery	Subtest	Definition	Example
Verbal	Verbal classification	Identify response word that best fits in the same category as stimulus word.	Dove Robin Sparrow Wren a. bee b. bat c. gull d. moth e. rabbit
	Sentence completion	Select a word that most appropriately completes the sentence.	Sue was very fond of her mathematics teacher but did not _____ her English teacher. a. obey b. like c. go to d. talk to e. see
	Verbal analogies	Select the word that best completes the verbal analogy.	*Bean* is to *pea* as *peach* is to a. tree b. apple c. fruit d. sun e. pit
Quantitative	Quantitative relations	Judgments are made about relative sizes or amounts.	I. 7 nickels II. 4 dimes Mark A if I is more money than II. Mark B if I is less money than II. Mark C if I is the same amount of money as II.
	Number series	Given a series of numbers, choose the number that comes next.	20 18 16 14 12 a. 11 b. 10 c. 9 d. 8 e. 7
	Equation building	Using numbers and symbols, construct the correct equation.	1 8 9 + − a. 0 b. 9 c. 10 d. 17 e. 18

Figure 6.1. Sample Items Like Those in the Cognitive Abilities Test

(*continued on the next page*)

SOURCE: Adapted from *Measurement and Evaluation in Psychology and Education* (6th ed.), by R. M. Thorndike. Copyright © 1997. Adapted with permission of Prentice-Hall, Inc., Upper Saddle River, NJ.

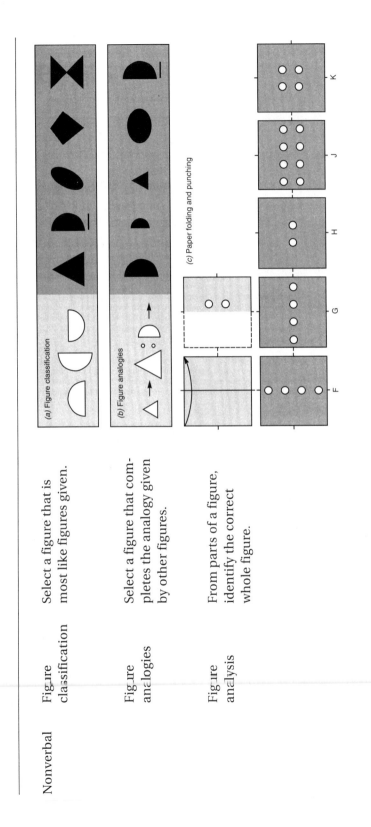

Nonverbal	Figure classification	Select a figure that is most like figures given.
	Figure analogies	Select a figure that completes the analogy given by other figures.
	Figure analysis	From parts of a figure, identify the correct whole figure.

(a) Figure classification

(b) Figure analogies

(c) Paper folding and punching

Figure 6.1. Continued

Some standardized aptitude assessments are designed to measure multiple abilities that are related to both academic and vocational success. The best-known example of this type of assessment is the Differential Aptitude Test Battery (DAT). There are eight tests in the DAT:

- Verbal aptitude
- Numerical ability
- Spatial aptitude
- Form perception
- Clerical perception
- Motor coordination
- Manual dexterity
- Finger dexterity

Because all the tests have been normed with the same group, the battery allows for the identification of students' strengths and weaknesses. Although the predictive power of the scores is not high, the results can be helpful in vocational counseling.

Individual Aptitude Assessments

An individual aptitude assessment is conducted by a trained test examiner with one examinee. It is an oral test administered face-to-face. The purpose of these assessments is the same as that of group aptitude tests—to measure abilities—but with a one-on-one administration, the results are usually more dependable and informative. The examiner can take into consideration such variables as examinee motivation, handicapping conditions, and persistence. These tests are used routinely in the identification of educational disabilities that qualify a student to receive special education services and placement in special programs.

Four commonly used individual aptitude assessments are summarized in Table 6.2. The Stanford-Binet Scale and Wechsler Scales have a long tradition of use in schools. Each of these scales is focused solely on abilities. Together, the scales provide global measures of intelligence in a few major areas. The Kaufman Assessment Battery and Woodcock-Johnson Psycho-Educational Battery–Revised are more recently developed tests that include both aptitude and achievement scales. The use of results from these two assessments is similar to that of the Stanford-Binet and Wechsler scales, but because there is a measure of achievement, more direct comparisons can be made between achievement and aptitude. This provides a more complete picture for diagnostic purposes. As with all standardized tests, each of the individual aptitude tests measures different skills. This makes it difficult to compare the scores from two or more of these tests. It also means that appropriate interpretations of the results occur only if it is clear what certain scores mean. This is best understood when those making the interpretations have knowledge about the nature of the specific items used in the test.

Administering Standardized Assessments

Because most standardized testing in schools takes place in classrooms, teachers will be responsible for administering them to students. It is important for the teachers to follow the directions carefully and explicitly. Instructions for the test administrators are provided in writing by the test publisher. These must be strictly followed, including any time limitations. Even if the teachers have administered similar tests in the past, the written directions should be read. The directions will indicate what to say to students, how to respond to student questions, and what to do while students are working on the test. Some portion of the instructions will probably direct the teachers to read directly from the instructions to the students, word for word as specified.

During the test, teachers may answer student questions about the directions or procedures for answering questions but should not help students in any way with an answer or what is meant by a question. Students should not be told to "hurry up" or "slow down." Teachers need to suspend their role as instructors and take on the role of test administrators. This isn't easy because most teachers want to help students do their best, especially with high-stakes tests that may reflect on the teacher. Whether the standardized assessment is national, state, or district in scope, the importance of strictly following directions can not be overemphasized.

While observing students as they take the test, teachers may see some unusual behavior or events that could affect the students' performance, such as interruptions or students acting out. These behaviors and events should be recorded for use in any subsequent interpretation of the results.

Preparing Students to Take Standardized Assessments

For students to do their best on standardized assessments, they need to have good test-taking skills. These skills help familiarize students with the format of the questions and give them strategies for answering the questions. These "test-wise" skills are important because they help to ensure validity of the inferences that are drawn from the results. That is, you don't want a situation in which students have done poorly, in part, because of a lack of test-taking skills. Here are some important test-taking skills that can be taught to students:

Table 6.2 Summary of Common Individual Aptitude Assessments

Stanford-Binet Scale, Fourth Edition	*Wechsler Intelligence Scale for Children—Revised (III)*	*Kaufman Assessment Battery for Children (K-ABC)*	*Woodcock-Johnson Psycho-Educational Battery—Revised*
Published in 1985, the fourth edition updates the content but retains the basic structure of previous editions. Given one-on-one to individuals 2 to 23, the test has 15 subtests grouped into four areas: quantitative reasoning, verbal reasoning, abstract/visual reasoning, and short-term memory.	Revised and restandardized in 1991, the WISC-III is designed for use with persons 6 to 16 years of age. Administered one-on-one, the WISC-III contains 10 subtests, 5 verbal and 5 performance.	Revised in 1983, the K-ABC provides a comprehensive assessment of both intelligence and achievement for children aged 3 to 12. Sixteen subtests are combined into three regularly administered scales. Intelligence is assessed with three scales. A measure of Mental Processing is obtained from the Simultaneous Processing and Sequential Processing Scales and achievement is assessed with the Achievement Scale.	Individually administered battery of tests to assess intelligence and academic achievement of individuals aged 4 through adulthood. Revised in 1989, the WJ-R contains a cognitive battery of 21 subtests (7 in the standard battery, 14 in the supplementary battery) to give a measure of intelligence, and 14 achievement subtests (9 in the standard battery, 5 in the supplementary battery).

- Read or listen to directions carefully.
- Read or listen to test items carefully.
- Set a pace that will allow adequate time to complete the test.
- Bypass difficult items and come back to them later (do easy items first).
- Make informed guesses, rather than omitting items.
- Eliminate as many options as possible before guessing.
- Follow directions for marking answers carefully.
- Check to be sure that the item number in the booklet matches the item number on the answer sheet.
- Check answers if time permits.
- Review item formats and strategies to get the answer.
- Look for grammatical clues to the right answer.
- Read all answers before selecting one.

It is also best to create an appropriate climate or classroom environment for taking the test. This begins with teachers' attitude toward the test. If the teachers convey to students that the test is a burden or an unnecessary or even an unfair imposition, students may adopt a similar attitude and may not try as hard as they can to do well. Teachers should impart an attitude of challenge and opportunity. Comments that add pressure or result in pretest jitters, such as saying what will happen if the scores are low, should be avoided. Teachers should emphasize to students that they should try to do their best and that this effort is more important than receiving a high score. Telling the students that the results are important and will be combined with other information will reduce anxiety, which could severely impair performance. If students appear overly anxious, their behavior should be noted to be included when interpreting the results. Some students may need counseling or other special services if test anxiety is serious.

Because most standardized tests use items that are fairly difficult, prepare students for this level of difficulty so that they are not easily discouraged. Give them practice items and short practice tests that simulate the difficulty of the items. Motivate students by explaining how the results will help them by improving teaching, learning, knowledge of themselves, and planning for the future.

A proper physical environment will support students' best efforts. Students need adequate work space, lighting, and ventilation. The room should be quiet, without distractions, and the test should be scheduled to avoid interruptions, such as school announcements. A sign such as Testing—Do Not Disturb should be placed on the door. The seating arrangement in the classroom should minimize distractions and cheating. Visual aids in the room that could help students should be removed. If possible, tests should be scheduled in the

Table 6.3 Teacher *Do*s and *Don't*s When Preparing Students
for Standardized Tests

Do	*Don't*
Teach to the test	Teach the test
Improve students' test-taking skills	Use the standardized test format for classroom tests
Establish a suitable environment	Describe tests as a burden
Motivate students to do their best	Tell students that important decisions will be made solely on the results of a single test
Explain why tests are given and how the results will be used	Use previous forms of the same test to prepare students
Give practice items and tests	Convey a negative attitude about the test
Tell students they probably won't know all the answers	
Tell students not to give up	
Tell students to skip and come back to hard items	
Allay student anxiety	
Have a positive attitude about the test	

SOURCE: Adapted from *Classroom Assessment: Principles and Practice for Effective Instruction* (2nd ed.), by J. H. McMillan, in press, Boston: Allyn & Bacon. Copyright © by Allyn & Bacon, Incorporated. Used with permission.

morning because students can usually focus better then than in the afternoon. Table 6.3 lists some *do*s and *don't*s regarding test preparation (adapted from McMillan, in press).

Interpreting Standardized Test Scores

On a standardized assessment, students answer questions and get a certain percentage of the items correct. As pointed out in Chapter 5, this is referred to as the student's *raw score*. Although some standardized tests report raw scores for subscales, the vast majority of scores that are used are modifications or transformations of the raw scores into *derived scores*. There are two types of derived scores, those that refer to the percentage correct, or *absolute derived score,* and those that are reported as a comparison with how others did on the same assessment, or *relative derived scores.* These two types of scores relate closely to criterion-referenced and norm-referenced interpretations, respectively. I will first examine norm-referenced scores that indicate relative position because these are the ones most commonly reported and most commonly misinterpreted.

Norm-Referenced Scores

Percentile Scores

One type of norm-referenced derived score, percentile, was introduced in Chapter 5. As a reminder: Percentile scores indicate the percentage of students in the reference group (norm group) who were outperformed. For example, a percentile score of 75 means that the student scored as well as or better than 75% of the students in the reference group. This gives meaning to the relative position of the score, but it does not tell much about the degree of difference between the scores. That is, the difference between scores of 80 and 85, in raw score units, is not the same as the difference between percentile scores of 50 and 55. This property makes it difficult to do much with percentiles beyond a simple description of results. For instance, because of unequal intervals, percentile scores should not be averaged.

Standard Scores

Standard scores are derived scores, transformed from raw scores, that are expressed as units of standard deviation. Each set of scores has a fixed or permanent mean and standard deviation with roughly equivalent units between the same number of scale points (e.g., a 5-point difference in performance means the same thing regardless of the location of the difference on the entire scale). This allows appropriate statistical analyses, such as averaging and comparing groups.

The simplest and most easily calculated standard score is the z score. A z score is expressed as units of standard deviation above or below the mean. The mean of the distribution is 0, and the standard deviation is 1. A z score can be calculated from any raw score as long as the mean and standard deviation of the raw score distribution is known:

$$z \text{ score} = (X - \overline{X})/SD$$

Where

X = any raw score

$\overline{X}$ = raw score distribution mean

SD = raw score distribution standard deviation

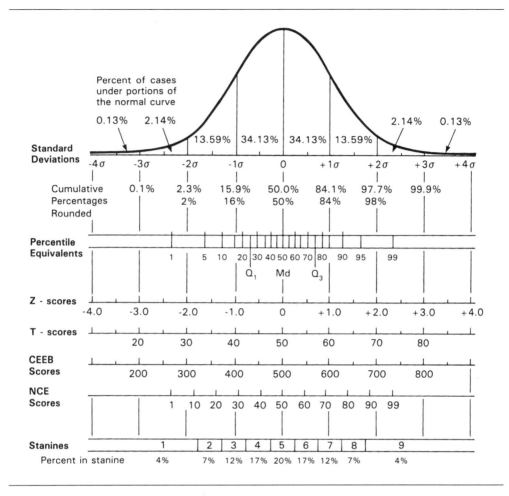

Figure 6.2. Normal Curve, Standard Deviations, Percentiles, and Selected Standard Scores

SOURCE: Reprinted from "Methods of Expressing Test Scores," by H. G. Seashore, in *Test Service Notebook No. 148*, September 1980, of The Psychological Corporation, a Harcourt Assessment Company. Copyright © 1980. Reprinted with permission.

For example, the *z* score for a raw score of 70 in a distribution that has a mean of 80 and a standard deviation of 10 is -1: (70 − 80)/10. Because the *z* score distribution has a standard deviation of 1, these scores can easily be transformed to other standard scores that will have only positive values. These are the types of standard scores reported with standardized tests. The new mean and standard deviation unit for the converted scores are usually determined arbitrarily, which can be confusing to the public. Different companies and states will adopt unique scales. Some of these are summarized in Figure 6.2 in relation to the normal curve and in Table 6.4.

Table 6.4 Types of Standard Scores

Standard Score	Description
Normal Curve Equivalent (NCE)	Scores range from 1 to 99, with a mean of 50 and a standard deviation of 21.06. NCEs are similar to percentile rank at the mean (50) and ends of the distribution (1 and 99). In between, however, NCEs are not equivalent to percentile.
T-score	Distribution with a mean of 50 and a standard deviation of 10.
Stanine	Scores that correspond to nine areas of the normal curve. The mean of the distribution is 5, with a standard deviation of about 2. There is a different percentage of scores in the range identified by each stanine.
Standard Age Score (also IQ scores)	Widely used with ability tests. The distribution has a mean of 100 and a standard deviation of 15 or 16.
Developmental Standard Score (growth score)	Allows year-to-year comparison of progress with a scale that is continuous across many grade levels (e.g., mean score at 2nd grade is 175; mean score at 4th grade is 200, and mean score at 6th grade is 225).
Scholastic Assessment Test (SAT)	Distribution with a mean of 500 and a standard deviation of 100 for quantitative and verbal tests.

Grade Equivalent Scores

A grade equivalent (GE) or grade norm score indicates student performance in relation to grade level and months of the school year, assuming a 10-month year. Thus, a GE of 4.6 refers to fourth grade, sixth month. As with other norm-referenced tests, GEs indicate a student's standing in relation to the reference group. The number is based on the performance of reference group students on the test at different grade levels. If the reference group of students in grade 4.6 achieved a mean score of 32 items correct, then any student who also got 32 items correct would receive a GE of 4.6. For a GE of 4.0, students would need to correctly answer less items, say 28.

GE scores appear to be easily interpreted because of the common sense referent to grade level (year and month in school). There are important limitations to these types of scores, however. Consider Tom, a third grader who obtained a GE score in mathematics of 4.7 at the beginning of the school year. Does this mean that Tom should be promoted to fourth grade, or that he could do as well as fourth graders, or that he is performing "above" grade level? The answer is no to each question. It can be said with confidence, however, that Tom has performed about the same on the test as students in the norming group who are in the seventh month of the fourth grade. Compared with other third graders in the reference group, Tom is above average, but his score does not imply that he would be successful with fourth-grade material or should be promoted to fourth grade.

GE scores are helpful in explaining student strengths and weaknesses. For example, consider Jennifer's scores in three areas during a 2-year period that includes fourth and fifth grades:

	4th Grade	*5th Grade*
Reading comprehension	5.6	5.8
Language	5.2	6.7
Mathematics	7.7	8.6

It is clear that relatively speaking, Jennifer is much stronger in mathematics than in either reading comprehension or language, that there is little difference between reading comprehension and language, and that her overall performance is above average when compared with the reference group. It is also clear that she is making good progress in language and mathematics but not in reading comprehension.

Although GE scores can be helpful in identifying strengths and weaknesses, and in examining growth, a number of important cautions limit what can be concluded from the scores.

1. It is incorrect to interpret the GE as the grade level at which the student is performing. That is, a GE of 7.2 for a fifth grader does not mean that the student is performing at the seventh-grade level; it means that the student is performing the same as a typical seventh grader taking the same test.

2. Most GE scores are extrapolated beyond and interpolated between the actual data provided by students in the reference group. For example, a sixth-grade test may be given to a sample of sixth graders only during the 2nd and 10th month of the year, yet scores are calculated to correspond to every month of the school year between these times (interpolated) and also calculated to correspond to GE scores prior to and after sixth grade (extrapolated). This means that many GE scores are only estimates of student performance.

3. A unit of 1 GE should not be the standard by which progress is evaluated. This assumes uniform growth throughout a year, when in reality, students learn at different rates.

4. GE scores do not indicate at what grade level students should be placed. Grade placement depends on local objectives and the performance of all students in the school. A third grader who scores a GE of 5.0 on a test shows strong mastery of the material, but this does not mean that skipping a grade would be appropriate.

5. Because GE scores are based on the normal distribution, half the students in the reference group are expected to be above the score and half below it. Expecting all students to be above grade level may not be consistent with the achievement levels of the students or local conditions. Above-average students (in comparison with the reference group) would be expected to achieve a GE score that places them "above" grade level, whereas a below-average class might be expected to simply reach the GE score that is consistent with their grade level.

6. Extremely high or low GE scores are problematic because of a lack of reliability for such scores and their heavy dependence on extrapolation.

7. The methods used to establish GE scores tend to exaggerate the importance of small differences in the number of items answered correctly.

8. GE scores from different tests cannot be compared because different tests of the same or similar content do not measure the same thing and because different reference groups will influence relative standing. Significant comparisons can be made only within the same test battery.

Standards-Based Scores

The second way scores are reported on standardized assessments is in relation to some standard, criterion, or level of performance. This criterion-referenced approach has been available for many years but was used only sporadically. Now that almost all states have developed learning standards or objectives and assess the extent to which students demonstrate competency that meets the standards and objectives, standards-based scores and criterion-referenced interpretations are common.

The basis for interpreting standards-based scores is the number of items answered correctly or the judgment of an expert who reviews a sample of student work, such as a writing sample. The raw score or expert judgment is used to determine placement into two or more categories, such as the following:

- Pass/fail
- Meets/fails to meet
- Advanced, proficient, basic, novice
- Not proficient, proficient, advanced
- Minimal, partial, satisfactory, extended
- No attempt, inadequate, satisfactory, competent, exemplary

The score that is reported corresponds to such categories, so meaning is directly dependent on what is meant by terms such as *pass* and *proficient* and *advanced*. Accurately interpreting the scores, then, requires understanding how the standards (or *benchmarks*) were set and what is meant by each level. Let's consider the most basic type of standard-based score—pass or fail. Suppose a school district has identified a set of fifth-grade mathematics competencies that must be demonstrated for students to obtain a passing score on the end-of-year fifth-grade mathematics test. Once the competencies have been identified, test items would need to be generated to measure the competencies. Suppose 20 questions are developed to measure each competency. How many of the 20 items would a student need to answer correctly to be judged competent? Seventy-five percent (15 correct of 20)? Half the items? Twelve items? Seventeen items? All 20 items? The determination of the standard involves making a judgment about the number of items that need to be answered correctly to classify the score as "pass." Who makes the judgment? Typically, such judgments are made by experts in the content area. They review the items and make decisions about whether students with competence in the area assessed would be able to answer the items. Of course, there is some variation in the judgments of different individuals, so usually there is some type of averaging of the judgments of many individuals.

A common approach to standards-based scores is to use a scale to report different levels of competency. For example, in the NAEP reports, a scale of 150 to 350 is used to correspond to different levels of performance. These scales are arbitrary and often are unique to a given test or state assessment program. In Virginia, for instance, scores on statewide competency tests, which are standards based, are reported using a scale of 0 to 600, with a score of 400 indicating proficient. The score indicating proficient stays the same for all content areas, although the number of items answered correctly is different.

Standards-based scores, then, depend not only on how well students do but also on the nature of the judgments made by those setting the standards. Accurate interpretations can be made only after inspecting the items and descriptions of what words such as *proficient* and *advanced* mean and by knowing about the individuals who set the standards. To promote accurate interpretations, standardized test developers release sample items and examples of student work that have been judged. These items can be reviewed to give some idea of the level of performance needed. The more removed the test is from a local setting, the more likely it is that those setting the standards will bring perspectives and values to that process that are inconsistent with local perspectives and values. National-level tests, such as the NAEP, are further from the classroom than a state test, and a state test is further from the classroom than a district test. Thus, those setting the standards on a national or state test are much less informed about local curriculum and values than those in the district who set standards only for schools and students in that district.

Difficulty of items is an important factor in standard setting, which is why sound inferences depend on knowledge of the items. There can be great variability in the difficulty of items that measure the same competency, objective, or standard. Given this variability, just knowing that a student answered 70% of the items correct is insufficient. You also need to know if these were hard or easy items! Obviously, getting 70% correct with easy items means something different from 70% with difficult items. One approach to judging the nature of the standard is to compare scores from the assessment with other performances of the students. This is essentially a check on the validity of the inferences drawn from the scores. It can provide a type of anchor for interpretation. For instance, suppose your brightest and highest-performing students don't "pass" the test. These are students who have demonstrated strong achievement in similar areas in class, yet they fail to show adequate performance. Because there is good evidence that they know the skills, it may be best to explore student motivation to do well on the test and to examine the test specifications and items in greater detail to determine a reasonable explanation for the discrepancy. It may be that what you thought was adequate knowledge and skill was not, or that the test is assessing areas you did not emphasize with your students.

As previously mentioned, many norm-referenced standardized tests purport to provide criterion-referenced information. Be wary of using norm-referenced tests in this way. It is best to use norm-referenced tests for what they are designed to do—show comparisons with other students, identify strengths and weaknesses, and show growth through time. To make sound decisions about whether students have obtained specific knowledge and skills, criterion-referenced assessments, which are designed for that purpose, are best.

One additional important limitation to most standardized assessments, both norm- and criterion-referenced, is the common use of a multiple-choice item format that allows machine scoring of student responses. This format, along with the need to be broad in coverage, results in the measurement of mostly low-level skills and knowledge (Marzano & Kendall, 1996). Such tests tend to assess isolated facts and only rudimentary understanding. Students select, rather than produce, a response on these types of tests. The multiple-choice format also gives the false impression that there is a right and wrong answer for all questions. Standardized tests encourage teaching of memorization, recall, and recognition, rather than application and other thinking skills.

One of the dilemmas of standards-based large-scale assessment is that if items are constructed to require application, analysis, synthesis, and other reasoning skills, the tests measure general ability in addition to knowledge and understanding of the content area. In Virginia, for example, the scores on the grade 8 English tests are strongly correlated to scores on both science and mathematics. Although incorporating reasoning skills with content may be desirable from one perspective, it complicates interpretation of the results from these assessments. If a student obtains a low score on a mathematics test that correlates strongly with performance in English, is the correct conclusion that the student is weak in mathematics or weak in applying math skills to these types of tests that require competence in reading comprehension to understand the question? Do low scores mean more work is needed in mathematics, in doing the types of items that are on the test, or in reading comprehension? As I have already stressed, the scores from these tests make most sense when interpreted in light of other indicators of student performance.

Interpreting Standardized Assessment Reports

Many types of reports can be produced from standardized assessments, including reports for parents, individual students, classes, schools, and school districts. Because the reports are designed to provide as much information as possible on a single page, they may appear complicated and difficult to understand. There is typically a large number of different scores, and often graphs are provided. For a comprehensive battery of tests, scores are usually reported for each skill as well as each subskill. A good approach to understanding the reports is to first consult the test manual and/or interpretation guide to find examples of explanations of actual scores. The manual or interpretation guide is also important for understanding the meanings of the labels used for the skills (e.g., math computation, measurement, and language). Most publishers of large-scale standardized assessments do a good job of explaining what each part of the report means.

Each test publisher has a unique format for reporting results and usually has unique types of scores. Different formats are used to summarize the scores. A single report may include a listing of all students in a class, the class as a whole, a skills analysis for the class or individual students, individual profiles, growth charts, and other formats. Some reports will include scores for only major content areas, whereas others will include subscale scores or even results for individual items. Also, different types of norms may be used. All this means that each report contains different information, organized and presented in unique formats. So the first step in understanding a report is to identify the nature of the information presented, then find an explanation for it in an interpretive guide.

Examples of two types of standardized test reports are illustrated in Figures 6.3 and 6.4. The individual profile report for a single student, Anne Stevens, is shown in Figure 6.3. The report summarizes results from a norm-referenced achievement test. Norm-referenced scores for 14 major content areas are provided at the top of the page, using both a national and local reference group. By comparing the local with national percentile scores, it is clear

(continued on p. 128)

Norm-Referenced Scores

Grade Equivalent	Normal Curve Equivalent	Scale Score	Local Percentile	Number Correct	National Percentile	NP Range	
2.5	42	590	5	21	36	27-46	Reading
2.9	43	585	10	11	38	28-49	Vocabulary
2.8	43	588	5	32	38	30-45	Reading Composite
2.8	42	602	8	13	36	25-48	Language
2.7	43	587	10	12	37	23-54	Language Mechanics
2.7	42	595	7	25	35	26-45	Language Composite
3.5	56	590	24	34	60	50-70	Mathematics
3.3	52	550	25	9	54	33-74	Math Computation
3.4	54	570	23	43	58	45-70	Math Composite
3.0	47	594	9	68	43	37-50	Total Score**
2.9	47	587	13	19	44	32-58	Science
3.8	57	613	21	22	64	53-73	Social Studies
2.7	38	541	8	6	29	18-42	Spelling
N/A	43	598	8	9	36	22-53	Word Analysis

** Total score consists of Reading, Language, Mathematics
N/A: No Score Available

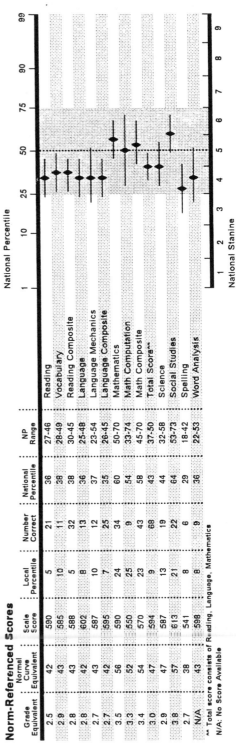

National Percentile

National Stanine

Performance on Objectives

National Stanine

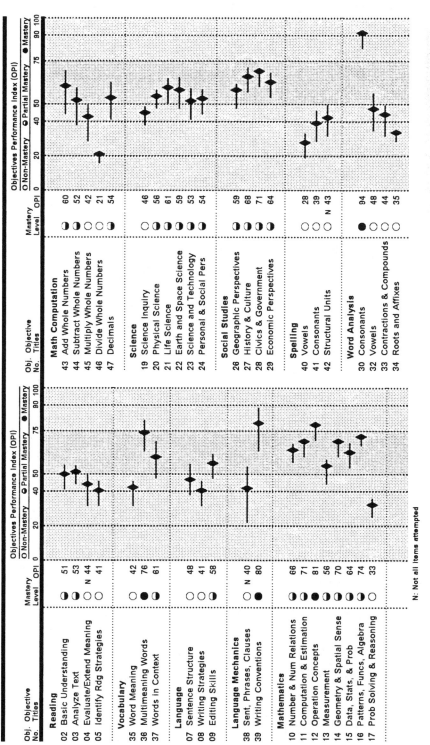

Figure 6.3. Example of Norm-Referenced Standardized Test Individual Report

SOURCE: *TerraNova: Individual Profile Report*, by CTB/McGraw-Hill, 1997, New York: McGraw-Hill. Copyright © 1997 by CTB/McGraw-Hill. All rights reserved. Reprinted with permission of The McGraw-Hill Companies, Inc.

Students	Scores	Read	Vocab	Read Cmpst	Lang	Lang Mech	Lang Cmpst	Math	Math Compu
ADKINS, LAURA M	NP	70	53	62	93	91	94	41	86
	GE	4.0	3.4	3.8	9.2	6.2	7.5	3.0	4.4
Birthdate: 07/21/87	NCE	61	52	57	82	78	83	45	73
Special Codes	SS	623	602	613	672	647	660	571	581
Student ID	LP	33	23	27	90	77	85	9	72
Other(K-T)	NCR	31	14	45	26	17	43	29	13
Form: A Level: 13									
BENCH, JENNIFER R	NP	90	*99	99	90	91	93	99	94
	GE	6.0	12.+	9.8	7.7	6.4	7.0	9.5	4.9
Birthdate: 11/15/87	NCE	77	99	98	77	79	80	99	83
Special Codes	SS	651	721	686	662	648	655	688	600
Student ID	LP	68	95	91	82	78	83	99	92
Other(K-T)	NCR	36	20	56	24	17	41	49	16
Form: A Level: 13									
CHOATE, DEBORAH M	NP	92	96	95	95	96	97	64	96
	GE	6.4	7.8	7.3	9.8	7.9	8.7	3.7	5.1
Birthdate: 01/31/88	NCE	79	86	84	84	86	89	58	86
Special Codes	SS	655	670	663	677	663	670	594	606
Student ID	LP	74	80	77	93	89	93	29	97
Other(K-T)	NCR	36	19	55	26	18	44	34	16
Form: A Level: 13									
CHU, LINDA B	NP	99	98	99	93	99	98	73	86
	GE	12.1	9.9	10.6	9.2	10.6	9.9	4.1	4.4
Birthdate: 04/22/88	NCE	99	95	99	82	96	94	63	73
Special Codes	SS	701	687	694	672	686	679	604	582
Student ID	LP	97	87	94	90	97	96	42	75
Other(K-T)	NCR	41	19	60	25	19	44	37	14
Form: A Level: 13									
CLAY, JILL M	NP	67	68	69	91	51	80	65	55
	GE	3.9	4.5	4.2	8.0	3.2	4.7	3.7	3.3
Birthdate: 03/29/88	NCE	60	60	60	78	51	68	58	53
Special Codes	SS	620	619	620	665	600	633	595	551
Student ID	LP	29	43	33	87	21	55	32	27
Other(K-T)	NCR	31	16	47	24	13	37	33	8
Form: A Level: 13									
CONNER, JENNIFER A	NP	82	74	79	87	96	94	89	96
	GE	4.9	4.8	4.9	7.3	7.9	7.5	5.2	5.1
Birthdate: 11/17/87	NCE	70	64	67	74	86	83	76	86
Special Codes	SS	637	626	632	657	663	660	627	605
Student ID	LP	50	49	50	75	89	85	75	96
Other(K-T)	NCR	34	16	50	24	18	42	41	15
Form: A Level: 13									

Individual Scores

NP:	National Percentile	** Total score consists of Reading, Language, Mathematics
GE:	Grade Equivalent	*: Maximum or Minimum score
NCE:	Normal Curve Equivalent	N/A: No Score Available
SS:	Scale Score	
LP:	Local Percentile	
NCR:	Number Correct	

Figure 6.4. Example of Norm-Referenced Standardized Test Class Report

SOURCE: *TerraNova: Class Record Sheet*, by CTB/McGraw-Hill, 1997, New York: McGraw-Hill. Copyright © 1997 by CTB/McGraw-Hill. All rights reserved. Reprinted with permission of The McGraw-Hill Companies, Inc.

Math Cmpst	Totl** Score	Sci	Social Stdy	Spell	Word Anlys
65	74	99	88	61	86
3.6	4.2	9.2	5.6	3.5	N/A
58	64	97	75	56	73
576	622	682	642	581	657
31	42	97	65	36	71
42	86	33	30	13	17
99	97	98	94	81	89
6.4	7.7	7.8	7.0	4.4	N/A
96	90	93	83	69	76
644	667	672	658	612	664
99	93	95	85	63	80
65	109	31	32	15	18
86	89	71	78	56	87
4.5	5.6	4.2	4.5	3.4	N/A
73	76	62	66	53	74
600	642	615	627	576	659
69	70	45	43	27	77
50	96	24	27	10	17
82	95	88	98	63	97
4.3	6.9	5.5	9.2	3.6	N/A
69	85	74	92	57	88
593	659	636	681	584	689
55	90	71	96	39	91
51	103	28	33	12	18
61	78	78	83	57	87
3.5	4.5	4.6	4.9	3.4	N/A
56	66	66	70	54	74
573	627	622	634	577	659
27	48	53	53	29	77
41	88	25	27	13	16
94	88	86	80	98	96
5.2	5.5	5.4	4.7	7.6	N/A
83	74	73	68	93	86
616	640	634	630	666	681
89	67	69	48	92	89
56	99	27	27	19	19

Figure 6.4. Continued

that Anne does much better in comparison with the national reference group than with other students in her district (local percentile). The number of items that were answered correctly and the national percentile range are also provided at the top of the page.

Many scores are reported, including grade equivalent, normal curve equivalent, a scale score, national percentile, and stanine. The chart shows the national percentile score along with a line on either side. The line represents the standard error of measurement, a range that represents where Anne's scores would lie if she took the test many times. The shaded area of the graph represents the average range of scores for the national sample. In reading, for example, Anne achieved a national percentile rank of 36. Compared with the national norm group, Anne is within the 25th to 75th percentiles on all the tests. The bottom section of the report shows how Anne performed on more specific "objectives." The Objectives Performance Index (OPI) is unique to this test. It provides an estimate of the number of items that a student could be expected to answer correctly if there had been 100 items for the objective. The OPI is also used to indicate "Mastery" (above 75), "Partial Mastery" (between 50 and 74), and "Nonmastery" (below 50). This is how this particular testing company, CTB/McGraw-Hill, provides information and an interpretation of student skills in fairly specific areas. Remember, however, that this interpretation depends on how difficult the items are and how closely the items match the content and skills taught. The Performance on Objectives section is a good example of how a norm-referenced assessment purports to provide criterion-referenced information. The procedure used to determine mastery and nonmastery, however, is arbitrary. Although the scores in this section appear to identify strengths and weaknesses (e.g., writing conventions and vowels are strengths, mathematics problem solving and dividing whole numbers are weaknesses), it would be helpful to know the number of items in each of these areas.

The report in Figure 6.4 shows a partial summary of students in a single class (there would be as many pages as needed to include all students). The same 14 major areas are included, with several types of scores shown for each student on each of the areas. This report is helpful to teachers because it provides a summary that allows comparisons among students and an efficient way to locate scores of all students. Because the scores reported do not include ranges that indicate error, any interpretation needs to take that into account. Observed scores such as those reported here are always, at best, an estimate of performance. Each student's "true" knowledge or skill could easily be higher or lower.

The results from this class illustrate the relationship between raw score (number of items correct) and percentile rank. Jill Clay answered 31 reading items correctly, which placed her in the 67th national percentile. Jennifer Conner answered three more items correctly (34), and this score was at the 82nd national percentile. In other words, answering three more items correctly resulted in a change of percentile rank of 15 points. In math, answering three more items correctly changed the percentile rank 9 points (Deborah Choate compared with Linda Chu). Overall, these students' scores "look better" if national norms are used. For every test, the national percentile is higher than the local percentile. This means that the locality, overall, scored higher than the national norm group.

Two examples of state-level standards-based reports are shown in Figures 6.5 and 6.6. The Virginia Student Performance Report shows scaled scores that are unique to these tests and a proficiency level summary for each of five major content areas. The reporting category scaled scores are also reported, ranging for Elizabeth Tomlinson from 31 to 44. The reporting category scores are not tied to proficiency levels and provide only a general idea of student strengths and weaknesses and a general indication of performance compared with other students statewide (35 is the state average). The reporting category scores do not add up to the total test score.

The Virginia School Summary Report (Figure 6.6) summarizes the number and percentage of students obtaining each of the four ratings in three writing domains. The mean scale scores for the test and reporting categories are indicated, as well as the number and percentage of students in the school who are categorized as fail/does not meet, pass/proficient, or pass/advanced. For this testing period, 38% of the students obtained a passing score. The written expression and usage mechanics scores show that these areas contribute in approximate equal amounts to the total score (62% show consistent or reasonable control for written expression; 65% show consistent or reasonable control in usage mechanics).

Using Standardized Assessment Results to Improve Instruction

The results of standardized testing can be used for planning prior to instruction and as a way to evaluate the effectiveness of instruction after content and skills have been taught. Any use of standardized scores should be done with the understanding that the results provide only one of many sources of information. Standardized test results should always be interpreted in the context of other evidence provided by classroom assessments and teacher observation. It is also important to understand the specific nature of the content or skills that are assessed.

Prior to instruction, results from standardized tests may provide a good indication of the general ability level of the students in the class. This information can be used to help establish reasonable, realistic expectations for students and to influence the nature of instructional materials. Expectations should not be fatalistically low or unreasonably high. If the results from a reading readiness test indicate that the class is lacking in ability to read, then

Virginia

Standards of Learning Assessments
STUDENT PERFORMANCE REPORT
GRADE 5 TESTS

Student ID#s are optional.

STUDENT NAME: ELIZABETH TOMLINSON
DOB: 10/24/85
GENDER: FEMALE
ID#   043156327690
ETHNICITY: WHITE
CLASS: M. SMITH
SCHOOL: LAKESIDE ELEMENTARY - 5678
DIVISION: NEWTOWN - 123

GRADE: 05
TEST DATE: SPRING 1998

TEST REPORTING CATEGORIES	# of ITEMS BLANK& MULTIPLE MARKED	SCALED SCORE	PROFICIENCY LEVEL SUMMARY
English: Reading/Literature and Research	0	433	PASS/PROFICIENT
Use word analysis strategies.	0	31	
Understand a variety of printed materials/resource materials.	0	35	
Understand elements of literature.	0	39	
Mathematics	0	406	PASS/PROFICIENT
Number and Number Sense	0	37	
Computation and Estimation	0	37	
Measurement and Geometry	0	39	
Probability and Statistics	0	33	
Patterns, Functions, and Algebra	0	35	
History and Social Science	0	361	
History	0	33	
Geography	0	33	
Economics	0	33	
Civics	0	33	
Science	0	400	
Scientific Investigation	0	32	
Force, Motion, Energy, and Matter	0	43	
Life Processes and Living Systems	0	34	
Earth/Space Systems and Cycles	0	30	
Computer/ Technology	0	484	
Basic Understanding of Computer Technology	0	43	
Basic Operational Skills	0	39	
Using Technology to Solve Problems	0	44	

Notes:

This *Student Performance Report* (SPR) displays scores for a student on all tests and their reporting categories except for *English: Writing,* which is reported on a separate SPR. The SPR shows, for each SOL test, the

- number of items to which the student did not respond (BLANK) and those where the student marked more than one answer (MULTIPLE-MARKED),
- scaled scores earned by the student on each test as a whole and its reporting categories, and
- proficiency level attained by the student (Pass/Advanced, Pass/Proficient, Fail/Does Not Meet).

Figure 6.5. Example of State Standardized Test Individual Report
SOURCE: Virginia Department of Education (1999).

the reading level of materials for the class needs to be carefully selected so that students can understand what they read. If it is clear that students have not mastered important prerequisites, then remedial instruction is needed. Individualization of instruction to students can be planned in part on the basis of test scores. Grouping can be determined in part from standardized test results. In cooperative learning, for example, it is common to group students so that all ranges of ability are represented in each group. Standardized tests,

Virginia
Standards of Learning Assessments
SCHOOL SUMMARY REPORT
GRADE 5
ENGLISH: WRITING

GRADE: 05
TEST DATE: SPRING 1998

SCHOOL: LAKESIDE ELEMENT..RY - 1234
DIVISION: NEWTOWN - 123

This is the number of students who earned a score on the test. It includes students who received a score of "0."

Mean Scaled Score for Total Test

Mean Scaled Scores for Reporting Categories

TEST REPORTING CATEGORIES	NUMBER/ PERCENT STUDENTS TESTED	NUMBER/PERCENT OF STUDENTS EARNING EACH DOMAIN SCORE				MEAN SCALED SCORE (MC + DW)	PROFICIENCY LEVEL SUMMARY Number and Percent in Each		
		Consistent Control	Reasonable Control	Inconsistent Control	Little or No Control		Fail/ Does Not Meet	Pass/ Proficient	Pass/ Advanced
ENGLISH: WRITING	71/93					**384.6**	44 62	24 34	3 4
Plan, compose, and revise in a variety of forms for a variety of purposes.						31.5			
Composing		10/ 14	32/ 45	27/ 38	2/ 3				
Written Expression		7/ 10	37/ 52	25/ 35	2/ 3			PERCENT PASSING = 38.0282	
Edit for correct use of language, capitalization, punctuation, and spelling.						31.1			
Usage-Mechanics		24/ 34	22/ 31	20/ 28	5/ 7				

Thirty-two students (45% of the students tested) received a rating of "reasonable control" in the composing domain on the direct writing component.

The percent of students tested is calculated by dividing the number of students tested by the number of students for whom an answer document was submitted (i. e., includes students who received a DNA because they were absent, exempted by their IEP, etc.)

Notes:

The *School Summary Report* (SSR) displays summary information on the Multiple-Choice and the Direct-Writing components of the *English: Writing* test. Included are
- number and percent of students earning each of the four possible ratings in each of the domains in the direct-writing component
- mean scaled score for each reporting category and for the total test
- percent of students passing, and
- number and percent of students attaining each proficiency level.

Figure 6.6. Example of State Standards-Based School Report
SOURCE: Virginia Department of Education (1999).

however, should not be the sole or even major determinant of instructional practices.

The scores in various subtests can be compared to identify strengths and weaknesses, which can help determine the amount of instruction to give in different areas. Students whose achievement is much lower than what might be expected on the basis of ability testing may need further testing, special attention, or counseling. What constitutes "much lower"? Generally, a discrepancy of 10 percentile points may be sufficient. If the percentile "bands" for achievement, which show the probable range of actual student knowledge or skill, do not overlap with the ability bands, then a significant discrepancy is identified.

Norm-referenced standardized tests are useful for selection and placement into special programs. This occurs at both ends of the achievement/aptitude distribution. Students are selected to receive special services in part on the basis of standardized test results; other students are placed in "gifted" programs or other advanced programs because they are identified as the brightest or most knowledgeable.

Standardized tests given at the end of instruction can be used to evaluate the effectiveness of instruction and curriculum. It is expected that students should score well in areas that have been stressed in the instructional program. If not, the scores act like a temperature gauge, indicating that further information needs to be gathered, such as other test performance data and a review of the match between specific standardized test items and subscales and what was taught. When standardized test data can be gathered through several years, it is possible to evaluate programs by examining trends in areas that have been emphasized and in areas that have not been the focus of instruction.

When students are tested each year, the scores can be used to indicate areas within the curriculum that need further attention. If an area shows a consistent pattern of low scores although the area is being stressed in the classroom, the specific methods of teaching may need to be examined.

Perhaps the most serious *misuse* of standardized tests is to evaluate teachers. This is a misuse of the results for several reasons: (a) Standardized tests are not designed to evaluate teaching or teachers; (b) the content and skills tested will not have a perfect match with local curriculum or what individual teachers stress in the classroom; (c) each year brings a unique group of students to a teacher, with knowledge, skills, motivation, and group chemistry that may be different from other years; (d) it is difficult, if not impossible, to isolate the influence of differences between teachers (most of what students experience is common); and (e) a standardized test provides only one indication of student performance.

In summary, most teachers will find standardized test results somewhat helpful *as long as the scores are used with a full understanding of their limitations and as a supplement to data gathered directly from students day to day.*

Often, these tests simply corroborate what teachers already know, but sometimes new information is provided that can have a positive influence on teaching practices. On a larger scale, to comprehensively evaluate programs and schools, standardized tests have value because of their technical soundness and their ability to identify strengths and weaknesses, show gains from year to year, and compare programs to establish effectiveness.

References

Airasian, P. W. (1997). *Classroom assessment* (3rd ed.). New York: McGraw-Hill.

Ames, C. (1992). Classrooms: Goals, structures, and student motivation. *Journal of Educational Psychology, 84,* 261-271.

Cizek, G. J. (1997). Learning, achievement, and assessment: Constructs at a crossroads. In G. D. Phye (Ed.), *Handbook of classroom assessment: Learning, adjustment, and achievement.* San Diego, CA: Academic Press.

Cizek, G. J., Rachor, R. E., & Fitzgerald, S. M. (1996). Teachers' assessment practices: Preparation, isolation, and the kitchen sink. *Educational Assessment, 3*(2), 159-179.

CTB/McGraw-Hill. (1997). *TerraNova: Individual profile report and class record sheet.* New York: McGraw-Hill.

Dweck,, C. S., & Leggett, E. L. (1988). A social-cognitive approach to motivation and personality. *Psychological Review, 95,* 256-273.

Frary, R. B., Cross, L. H., & Weber, L. J. (1993). Testing and grading practices and opinions of secondary teachers of academic subjects: Implications for instruction in measurement. *Educational Measurement: Issues and Practice, 12*(3), 23-30.

Gardner, H. (1993). *Multiple intelligences: Theory into practice.* New York: Basic Books.

Heubert, J. P., & Hauser, R. M. (Eds.). (1999). *High stakes testing for tracking, promotion, and graduation.* Washington, DC: National Academy Press.

Impara, J. C., & Plake, B. S. (1996). Professional development in student assessment for educational administrators. *Educational Measurement: Issues and Practice, 15*(2), 14-19.

Linn, R. L., & Gronlund, N. E. (1995). *Measurement and assessment in teaching* (7th ed.). Englewood Cliffs, NJ: Merrill/Prentice Hall.

Marzano, R. J., & Kendall, J. S. (1996) *A comprehensive guide to designing standards-based districts, schools, and classrooms.* Alexandria, VA: Association for Supervision & Curriculum Development.

McLaughlin, G. H. (1969). SMOG: Grading a new readability formula. *Journal of Reading, 21,* 620-625.

McMillan, J. H. (1999a). *Teachers' classroom assessment and grading practices: Phase 1.* Richmond, VA: Metropolitan Educational Research Consortium, Virginia Commonwealth University.

McMillan, J. H. (1999b). *Teachers' classroom assessment and grading practices: Phase 2*. Richmond, VA: Metropolitan Educational Research Consortium, Virginia Commonwealth University.

McMillan, J. H. (in press). *Classroom assessment: Principles and practice for effective instruction* (2nd ed.). Boston: Allyn & Bacon.

McMillan, J. H., & Schumacher, S. (1997). *Research in education: A conceptual introduction* (4th ed.). New York: Longman.

Mehrens, W. A., & Lehmann, I. J. (1987). *Using standardized tests in education* (4th ed.). White Plains, NY: Longman.

Messick, S. (1989). Validity. In R. L. Linn (Ed.), *Educational measurement* (3rd ed.). New York: American Council of Education/Macmillan.

Messick, S. (1995). Validation of inferences from persons' responses and performances as scientific inquiry into score meaning. *American Psychologist, 50,* 741-749.

National Assessment of Educational Progress. (1999). *NAEP 1998 reading report card for the nations and states*. Washington, DC: U.S. Department of Education, National Center for Education Statistics, Office of Educational Research and Improvement.

Payne, D. A. (1997). *Applied educational assessment*. Belmont, CA: Wadsworth.

Phelps, R. P. (1998). The demand for standardized student testing. *Educational Measurement: Issues and Practices, 17*(3), 5-23.

Pintrich, P. R., & Schunk, D. H. (1996). *Motivation in education: Theory, research, and applications*. Englewood Cliffs, NJ: Prentice Hall.

Popham, W. J. (1995). *Classroom assessment: What teachers need to know*. Boston: Allyn & Bacon.

Popham, W. J. (1997). Consequential validity: Right concern—wrong concept. *Educational Measurement: Issues and Practice, 16*(2), 9-13.

Seashore, H. G. (1980). Methods of expressing test scores. In *Text service notebook 148*. New York: Psychological Corporation.

Shepard, L. A. (1997). The centrality of test use and consequences for test validity. *Educational Measurement: Issues and Practice, 16*(2), 5-8, 13, 24.

Standards for teacher competence in educational assessment of students. (1990). Washington, DC: National Council on Measurement in Education.

Sternberg, R. J. (1985). *Beyond IQ: A triarchic theory of intelligence*. Cambridge, UK: Cambridge University Press.

Stiggins, R. J., & Conklin, N. F. (1992). *In teachers' hands: Investigating the practices of classroom assessment*. Albany: State University of New York Press.

Thorndike, R. M. (1997). *Measurement and evaluation in psychology and education* (6th ed.). Upper Saddle River, NJ: Prentice Hall.

Tombari, M. L., & Borich, G. D. (1999). *Authentic assessment in the classroom: Applications and practice*. Upper Saddle River, NJ: Merrill/Prentice Hall.

Virginia Department of Education. (1999). *Standards of learning assessments*. Richmond: Author.

Whittington, D. (1999). Making room for values and fairness: Teaching reliability and validity in the classroom context. *Educational Measurement: Issues and Practice, 18*(1), 14-22, 27.

Wood, J. (1992). *Adapting instruction for mainstreamed and at-risk students* (2nd ed.). Upper Saddle River, NJ: Prentice Hall.

Index

CORWIN
PRESS

The Corwin Press logo—a raven striding across an open book—represents the happy union of courage and learning. We are a professional-level publisher of books and journals for K–12 educators, and we are committed to creating and providing resources that embody these qualities. Corwin's motto is "Success for All Learners."